COOKING with CARE

COOKING with CARE

OCTOPUS BOOKS

ACKNOWLEDGEMENTS

Photography by Martin Brigdale, assisted by Nick Carman

Photographic styling by Hilary Guy

Food prepared for photography by Janice Murfitt

Editor: Moyra Fraser

Art Editor: Alyson Kyles

Designer: Sue Storey

Home Economists: Carole Handslip
Anna James
Janice Murfitt

p. 50 Did You Know . . . ? facts supplied by Mari Roberts

p. 36/37 Tableware courtesy of Wedgwood at Oxford Circus, London W1

Front cover
Chicken and lemon risotto (page 24)
Avocado with grapes (page 62)
Vanilla cheesecake (page 38)

Back cover
Honey stickjaws (page 54)
Tug-boat eggs (page 52)
Sweetcorn tartlets (page 52)

First published 1986
© Octopus Books Limited 1986

ISBN 0 7064 2664 9

Produced by Mandarin Publishers Ltd
22a Westlands Road
Quarry Bay, Hong Kong

Printed in Hong Kong

CONTENTS

EATING and HEALTH

For most of us, the *you are what you eat* approach to nutrition is far too extreme to swallow whole but there's certainly no doubt that diet plays a key role in staying fit. What we eat has a profound effect not just on our figures and the way we look but, much more importantly, on our health – right now and in years to come.

The million dollar question, of course, is what sort of diet should we be following? Fortunately, we can forget the fads and fancies of the past and throw out the high-protein, low-carbohydrate, grapefruit-before-every-meal variations because what has emerged in the '80s is an exciting, new idea about nutrition. Clear dietary guidelines have been formulated by a group of top medical and food experts in order to help us all to eat more healthily. This group, called the National Advisory Committee on Nutrition Education (NACNE) has made easy guide-lines on food that we can all follow. There's no need for a drastic change in lifestyle, simply adapt eating habits to fit in with the four main recommendations. Essentially, these are embodied in four messages: *eat less fat, but especially saturated fat, cut down on sugar, be sparing with the salt* and *eat more fibre.*

There's no need to be faddish to feel fit!

What exactly are the dangers we're trying to avoid and the benefits we aim to grasp? Research has shown that a healthy diet can reduce the risk of heart disease and help prevent overweight, tooth decay and a whole range of other disorders. Of course, other factors such as exercise and whether or not you smoke contribute to these so-called 'diseases of affluence' but for positive good health, vitality and a sense of well-being we really cannot afford to leave diet to chance. It is worth getting into a healthier pattern of eating.

Raw Health. Clockwise from the top: Ingredients for Gingered apricot compote (recipe page 43); Pilaff of pork (recipe page 31); Italian pasta salad (recipe page 36); Vegetable curry (recipe page 33) (see page 11 for finished dishes).

FACTS about FATS

Cut down on fat, especially saturated fat. This is probably one of the easiest recommendations to adopt since few of us have a craving for fat in the same way as many of us long for sweet foods or salty, savoury snacks and because there are now plenty of low-fat alternatives to full-fat foods on the market. Skimmed milk, for instance, has almost all its fat removed while many new low-fat cheeses have half the fat (and calories) of the traditional product. When it comes to the main meal, choose white fish, lean red meat, chicken or turkey. Other excellent sources of both protein and fibre, not loaded down with fat, are dried beans, peas and lentils, all of which make delicious and economical alternatives. Watch out for the hidden sources of fat, though. Biscuits, cakes, crisps, pastry and chocolate as well as cream are all high in fat and most of it is saturated.

Many people are confused by all the different types of fat — vegetable and animal. All fats are made of a mixture of saturated and unsaturated fatty acids. Which type predominates depends on the source of the fat. A rough guide as to whether a fat is mostly saturated or unsaturated is its hardness at room temperature. Butter for example is fairly hard and contains about 60% saturated fat, a block margarine around 40% but soft margarine made with pure vegetable oil (such as sunflower) is about 15-20% saturated fat.

PASS the SALT

Although essential to life, it is now suggested that we consume far too much salt and should cut back from our current level. Theoretically, any surplus salt will be excreted via the kidneys, but some people cope with an excess better than others. It has been found that some of us are very susceptible to the salt in our diets and a high intake may raise our blood pressure and lead to further problems.

A great deal of the salt we eat is found in manufactured foods like prepared convenience foods, processed meats, cheese and bacon. In fact, a packet of potato crisps alone contains 1g of salt and a Chinese takeaway even more! However, as much as one third of the salt we consume comes from the amount we add to food ourselves. How many of us are guilty of automatically placing the

A SPOONFUL of SUGAR

Sugar hasn't managed to gain the seal of approval in terms of health. Although it hasn't been condemned as the cause of coronary heart disease, sugar has been shown to contribute to our dental problems. Not only do dentists advise children to look after their teeth but they also encourage them to avoid sugary foods and drinks between meals.

If you have a weight problem, you should consider cutting back on foods and drinks with a high sugar content. Although not extremely calorific, sugar forms an unnecessary part of our diet. Other foods not only provide the fuel we require but also essential nutrients. Help get your diet in shape when buying food by reading food labels and avoiding those foods laden with sugar.

Sugar appears in many forms both visible and invisible. We may not take sugar in tea or coffee but many manufactured foods such as certain breakfast cereals, biscuits and cakes are high in

FOCUS on FIBRE

Dismissed for years as useless, roughage or dietary fibre as it 'has been re-christened, is now recognized as an essential part of a healthy diet. Fibre is found not only in cereals such a wheat, oats and rye but also in fruit and vegetables, nuts and seeds plus dried beans and lentils. Although fibre is found in all these foods, our diets are still low in fibre. So how can fibre help? When food passes through the digestive system the fibre part is not digested. This bulk or roughage is highly water absorbent and helps remove waste products through the system. Without this 'removal pro-

Saturated fat

Roughly one fifth of our daily calorie intake comes from harder saturated fats and the reason this proportion needs to be reduced sharply is that this particular type of fat may be implicated with the cause of coronary heart disease. Evidence shows that a diet high in saturated fat can push up the level of fatty substances in the blood (including cholesterol) which in turn furs up the arteries and could lead to a heart attack. Most of the saturated fats we eat are found in animal products including beef, lamb, pork and lard as well as dairy products like milk, cheese, butter and hard margarine. The two main exceptions are coconut and palm oil which, although of vegetable origin, are enormously high in saturated fat.

Polyunsaturated fat

This type of fat is actually needed for health as it includes *essential* fatty acids. Polyunsaturated fat is found mostly in vegetable oils such as sunflower, corn, soya and safflower plus oily fish like mackerel and trout. The soft margarines which are labelled 'high in polyunsaturates' must contain high levels of this type of fat as well as low levels of saturated fat. Results of many studies have shown that, unlike saturated fat, polyunsaturates do *not* increase blood cholesterol level and indeed may even help reduce it. So, when it comes to cutting down on fat, it's mainly the saturated sort that should be reduced while replacing some of it with polyunsaturates.

salt cellar on the table as we lay it, and salting our food even before we have tasted it? Try to reduce the amount sprinkled on during cooking and keep the salt cellar off the table.

sugar. The sugar found in natural foods such as fruit and vegetables is combined with valuable nutrients and we are much less likely to 'overdose' or develop sweet cravings if our sugar intake comes mainly from these natural sources.

cess' a diet low in fibre has been shown to be associated with disorders such as constipation, diverticulitis and other bowel diseases.

WHAT DO YOU KNOW?

Try these questions to test your knowledge of food facts and fallacies. The answers are on page 79.

1 Which of the following should we cut down to help reduce the risk of heart disease?
- a) Dietary fibre
- b) Saturated fat
- c) Polyunsaturated fat

2 Are any of the following high in saturated fat?
- a) Salami
- b) Baked Beans
- c) Double cream
- d) Cottage cheese

3 Which two of the following foods are high in polyunsaturated fat?
- a) Egg yolks
- b) Butter
- c) Oily fish
- d) Soft margarine made with sunflower oil

4 Which of the following factors can increase the risk of heart disease?
- 1) Smoking
- 2) Lack of exercise
- 3) High blood pressure

5 Which of these old wives' tales has any truth?
- a) Carrots make you see in the dark
- b) Large doses of vitamin C will help prevent the common cold

6 Aduki, mung, cannellini, barlotti, flageolet . . . these are all varieties of which kind of food?
- a) Pasta
- b) Dried beans
- c) Curry spices

7 If you cut down on your sugar intake, you will lose some of your energy and feel lethargic. **True or False?**

8 What will ensure that we are eating enough dietary fibre?
- a) Adding bran to our foods
- b) Eating plenty of fresh fruit and vegetables every day
- c) Using more cereals, peas and beans and lentils in our cooking

9 Is it true that grapefruit or lemon juice taken before a meal will help the body to use up fat more quickly? **Yes or No?**

10 To reduce weight quickly it is a good idea to cut out bread, potatoes and pasta? **True or False?**

A PRACTICAL GUIDE

Knowing the benefits of a healthy diet, how do we put our good intentions into practice? To eat healthily is not 'a bother', and no one is suggesting that we change the habits of a lifetime overnight! With very little effort we can do a lot to improve our diets simply by making small, gradual adjustments to our normal, everyday meals. The advice is simple and enjoyable to follow. To get into a healthier pattern of eating we should gradually try to:

Use less of some foods and more of others e.g. less fatty meat and meat products and more poultry and fish.

Choose healthier varieties of our regular foods e.g. skimmed, or semi-skimmed milk rather than full-cream milk, and margarines high in polyunsaturates rather than butter.

Introduce 'new' ingredients to our cooking e.g. wholemeal pastas, pitta bread, aubergines and so on.

For most people, shopping for food is an inevitable chore. In supermarkets especially there's always a great temptation to fill up the trolley and be out through the checkout as quickly as possible. However, we cannot produce healthier meals unless the right ingredients are ready to hand. So the next time you go shopping make a fairly detailed list, preferably for a week's menus, and bear in mind the following checklist.

Help Yourself to Health

Greengrocer

Buy plenty of fresh fruit and vegetables; at least two portions of fruit and two portions of vegetables or salad per person per day.

For the best value, choose whatever's in season and remember that market stalls and pick-your-own farms are often cheaper.

Only choose produce in good condition, nothing old and wilted, but don't be put off by odd shapes or small blemishes. Bruised melon and pineapple, for example, will still make excellent fruit salads and toppings for cheesecakes and flans.

The selection of fresh fruit and vegetables available today is greater than ever before. Take time to look at the more exotic varieties and pick up the information leaflets giving preparation and cooking advice.

Healthy Hints

● Get into the habit of serving an extra vegetable or side salad with your main course.
● Keep the fruit bowl full with seasonal fruits for a refreshing addition to breakfast, to pop into lunch boxes, or to enjoy after meals.
● Take advantage of the abundance of soft fruits such as strawberries, when in season. This is the time to stock the freezer with whole fruit, fruit purées and home-made sorbets for delicious desserts throughout the year.
● Home-grown vegetables or produce bought from pick-your-own farms make economical and useful additions to the freezer.
● Remember that many vegetables, such as courgettes and carrots, can be thinly sliced or coarsely grated into salads.

Bakery

Choose more wholemeal bread and high-fibre white bread and try some of the speciality breads such as wholemeal baguette, pitta and rye bread. Try and include bread in every meal.

If you're on the look out for something different for teatime and you don't have time to do some baking, try wholemeal scones, muffins and tea breads.

Healthy Hints

● Wholemeal breadcrumbs form the base of excellent stuffings for fish, chicken, turkey and vegetable dishes.
● Give a crunchy, nutty topping to otherwise soft-textured dishes like lasagne by adding a layer of wholemeal breadcrumbs and toasted sunflower, sesame or pumpkin seeds before baking.

Fishmonger

Each week, plan to have at least one meal with fish. It's delicious, it's healthy, it's easily digested – and it's always excellent value for money. It also cooks rapidly and lends itself to a wide range of possibilities from simple grilling to nourishing pies.

It doesn't matter whether you patronize a favourite fishmonger's shop, a market stall or the fish counter of a big supermarket as long as supplies are good, fresh and varied. Always approach fish counters with an open mind and a flexible shopping list. If the variety you want is unavailable, or expensive, be prepared to substitute another variety with a similar texture e.g. haddock or coley for cod.

Healthy Hints
- When poaching fish, experiment with different flavourings in the poaching water e.g. sprigs of rosemary or thyme, crushed cardamom pods, slices of lime or orange. The strained liquid can then be used to make a delicious sauce to accompany the fish.

Butcher

Poultry is a very economical source of lean meat. Both chicken and turkey are especially lean, and very useful for main meal dishes, salads and sandwiches.

Meat is a good source of protein, minerals and vitamins but a small amount can provide all we require. All meat has fat on it, or in it, even fillet steak.

When buying meat choose the leaner cuts such as topside, stewing steak or pork tenderloin and don't forget liver and kidney. Remember to cut all visible fat from meat before cooking. Buy the best quality mince – look for the supermarket packs labelled 'lean'. If possible, at the butcher's, choose a piece of meat

and ask the butcher to mince it for you.

Lamb tends to be a fatty meat, especially breast and shoulder. Choose leg of lamb for roasting and loin chops in preference to neck and chump chops.

Sausages and other meat products like hamburgers, pies, pasties, salami and corned beef are all high in saturated fat so try to buy them less often.

Healthy Hints
- When casseroling chicken, remove the skin before cooking. If roasting, remove after cooking.
- Use less red meat in casseroles. Bulk up quantity with extra vegetables or dried fruits such as apricots or prunes.

Dried Foods

Dried foods form the basis for a range of interesting and economical meals. Pasta makes for very cheap meals. Look for a type of pasta you haven't used before such as fresh tagliatelle or wholemeal pasta shells and serve with your next casserole or stew.

Keep a good stock of rice in the larder. Both long- and round-grain varieties of brown rice are now available.

Stock up too on dried peas, beans and lentils for soups, salads and savouries.

For quick meals and snacks bulgar wheat is invaluable. It can be ready to use in salads in 15 minutes or quickly cooked to serve hot in 10 to 12 minutes.

For salads, simply soak the wheat in enough cold water to cover and leave for about 15 minutes or until the grains are swollen and tender, and the water completely absorbed. Stir in any combination of ingredients such as chopped herbs, tomatoes, peppers, onions, cooked chopped chicken or turkey etc., and moisten with a little French dressing with herbs for a delicious salad (see page 77).

To serve hot, cover with cold water and bring to the boil. Simmer gently for 10 to 12 minutes. Drain well and serve

as you would rice or pasta.

Dried fruits are extremely versatile ingredients to have on hand for both sweet and savoury dishes. They are a very rich source of vitamins, minerals and important dietary fibre. An excellent snack at any time of the day, especially for children.

The basic ingredients for muesli are found in most supermarkets now so keep rolled oats, nuts, sunflower and sesame seeds in stock as well as dried fruits. Encourage children to make up their own favourite recipe.

If you're buying ready-made muesli look for the ones with no added sugar.

Switch to buying wholemeal flour to increase fibre in your cooking and baking and to add a delicious, nutty flavour.

Healthy Hints
- Brown rice does take longer to cook but can be cooked in advance and reheated in 25 to 30 minutes if tightly covered in a lightly greased dish and placed beneath a casserole in a moderate oven.
- Soak and cook peas, beans and lentils in large batches. Freeze in useful portions (see Bean Cuisine page 30). Add to soups and stews straight from the freezer.

Canned Foods

If buying canned fruits choose the varieties canned in 'own juice' or in apple or pear juice rather than syrup. Apart from cutting calories you will enjoy the natural fruit flavour.

Stock up with a selection of canned beans and peas. They are a good standby to have in the larder. Remember to rinse them well before using.

Select canned fish such as mackerel, tuna and sardines in brine or tomato sauce rather than oil.

Many vegetables are now canned in unsalted water. Look out for 'No Added Salt' on the label.

Cooking Fats and Oils

Dripping, suet, lard and most white fats are all saturated fats and best avoided. Try to reduce the amount of fried food you eat but if you do fry use a polyunsaturated oil or a fat labelled 'high in polyunsaturates'.

Healthy Hints
• Always strain cooking oil after deep-fat frying. When it has been used three or four times change to fresh oil.
• Always drain fried foods on absorbent kitchen paper before serving.

Seasonings

Keep a selection of different herbs and spices in store to 'season' foods rather than always using salt. This way the true flavour of foods can be appreciated.

Mixers and Squashes

Choose the 'low-calorie' or 'sugar-free' varieties of lemonades and squashes. Try mixing sparkling mineral water with pure, unsweetened fruit juice for a refreshing drink.

Cool Cabinet

Edam, Brie and Feta cheeses are all excellent choices for cooking and for the cheeseboard. Try too, the low-fat alternatives to the hard, Cheddar-type cheeses. There is an increasing variety of soft cheese to choose from.

Opt too, for the low-fat yogurts and try smetana. This is a cross between soured cream and yogurt but with less fat than soured cream (see page 77 for a recipe for home-made smetana).

Healthy Hints
• Always choose margarines and cooking fats labelled 'high in polyunsaturates' for spreading, cooking and frying.

Consider the following hints and tips when planning your next meals.

Grilled to perfection

Grilling is an excellent way of cooking meat, fish, poultry and certain vegetables (mushrooms, courgettes, tomatoes, aubergines etc.). It's a much healthier alternative to frying and just as quick and easy.

A good marinade will make all the difference to taste and texture, producing food that is tender and full of flavour. Leave the food in the marinade for at least 1 hour and preferably overnight. The basic ingredients for a marinade are sunflower oil, lemon, wine or wine vinegar, herbs and spices. A marinade of natural yogurt, garlic, sunflower oil and curry spices over chicken drumsticks

Cooking for Health

will produce a delicious home-made tandoori (see page 51).

Stir Fry

If you do fry, use a non-stick pan and sunflower oil. Woks too are ideal for frying.

One Pot Meals

Casseroles and stews are best prepared the day before to allow the flavours time to develop. This also allows the excess fat to be skimmed off the surface with a spoon or absorbent kitchen paper before reheating or packing away.

Roasting Rules

Cook meat and poultry on a rack over a roasting tin so the fat drips underneath. Skim the fat off with absorbent kitchen paper before using the juices for gravy.

Remove any fat from inside poultry before roasting. Prick all over with a fork to allow the fat to run out as it cooks.

Vegetable Variations

The valuable vitamins in vegetables are quickly destroyed once the vegetables are peeled and cut surfaces are exposed to air or soaked in water. Therefore try not to prepare them too far in advance and don't overcook. As far as possible don't peel either as this will remove the valuable fibre in the skin.

If vegetables are to be boiled use the minimum amount of water or stock and cook until just tender.

Try steaming or microwaving a variety of vegetables such as strips of celery, carrot and courgette for an accompaniment full of colour, flavour and texture.

Salad Suggestions

Vary the content of salads according to the season and experiment with more unusual ingredients. Try combining fruit with vegetables such as orange segments with grated carrot, chopped apple with celery and so on.

Just Desserts

Start questioning the quantity of sugar given in recipes. Home-made ice-creams, mousses and custards, for example, often taste better when the sweetness is reduced.

Try substituting natural yogurt for all or half the cream whenever possible. Some cold soufflés set with gelatine can be made just as successfully with all natural yogurt instead of whipping cream (see pages 38 and 39) or half yogurt and half cream.

Sauces and Custards

In any recipe for a milk and flour-based sauce, e.g. bechamel or custard, the whole milk can be successfully replaced with skimmed milk.

Left: Caramelized grapefruit
(recipe page 16)

A simple recipe but very effective
and one which can be used on
many occasions. Serve as a light
starter before a fairly heavy main
course or, as we have suggested
here, as a refreshing start to the
day.

EVERYDAY COOKING

Producing nourishing, tasty and popular meals on a day-to-day basis is no easy task, especially when time is often at a premium and ideas are running thin. All the basic foods we require for a healthy diet are readily available, so all that's needed are plenty of imaginative ideas to ring the changes and make our everyday meals more exciting and nutritious. The recipes given here do just that. They are designed to make the job of cooking good food a pleasure, not a chore.

Casseroles and warming soups are a good choice for lunch and supper dishes as they can be prepared ahead and are easily kept hot until required. Serve with salads, lightly cooked vegetables or wholemeal bread for a satisfying meal.

Tasty risottos and pilaffs made with rice or quick-cooking bulgar wheat make easy meals with very little effort. Remember to include more fish and offal when planning meals. They rarely take longer than 10 to 15 minutes to cook. A stack of marinated Saffron Seafood Kebabs, for example, can be ready and waiting in the refrigerator to grill to order later that day (recipe page 24).

It's a good idea to get into the habit of cooking double batches of rice, beans and pulses. They will keep, covered in the refrigerator for 2 to 3 days (or frozen in handy portions, see Bean Cuisine page 30) ready to be added to salads for a light meal, or stirred into soups and stews.

A large bowl of seasonal fruits is the simplest and freshest ending to a meal but the occasional pudding is still on the menu too. Tempting fruit pies, crumbles and feather-light sponges are simple to make and delicious served with light custards and sauces. Chilled and frozen desserts can be made well in advance. Yogurt-based ice creams will be just right for serving if they are transferred to the refrigerator when the main course is served.

Home-made cakes, biscuits and scones can be batch-baked and stored in airtight containers or in the freezer. They are ideal to have on hand to add to picnics or lunch boxes. They can also be served with stewed fruits and yogurt for an impromptu pudding.

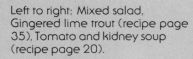

Left to right: Mixed salad, Gingered lime trout (recipe page 35), Tomato and kidney soup (recipe page 20).

Eating well doesn't mean spending hours in the kitchen preparing elaborate meals. However, it does make sense to plan ahead and choose dishes such as this main meal soup which can be left unattended or recipes which will involve very little last minute preparation such as this quick and easy fish dish which only takes 30 minutes from start to finish.

Right: Gooseberry and elderflower sherbet (recipe page 40).

An attractive end to any meal and a handy standby to have in the freezer. Remember to transfer the sherbet to the refrigerator about 20 minutes before serving.

BAKED FRUIT COMPOTE

SERVES 4

250 g/8 oz dried apricots
125 g/4 oz dried, pitted prunes
600 ml/1 pint cold tea
125 g/4 oz sultanas
2 small bananas, thickly sliced
1 large orange

Place the apricots and prunes in a bowl and pour over the tea. Cover and leave to soak overnight.

Stir in the sultanas and bananas. With a serrated knife, peel the orange of all skin and pith. Cut down between the membranes to release the orange segments. Stir into the fruit mixture.

Cover and bake in a preheated oven (190°C/375°F, Gas Mark 5) for about 30 minutes. Serve hot with Home-made Yogurt.

This compote can also be made with pure, unsweetened apple or orange juice instead of tea.

● high fibre	300 calories
● low saturated fat	P:S ratio 1:1

CARAMELIZED GRAPEFRUIT

SERVES 4

2 pink grapefruit
demerara sugar
pinch grated nutmeg
15 g/½ oz Flora margarine

Cut the grapefruit in half, horizontally, then using a serrated grapefruit knife, loosen the segments. Discard the pips and cut out the centre core. Arrange the grapefruit on a baking tray. Sprinkle with a little sugar and nutmeg. Dot each one with margarine.

Place in a preheated oven (200°C/400°F, Gas Mark 6) for 15 to 20 minutes. Alternatively, place under a hot grill for 4 to 5 minutes until golden brown. Serve immediately garnished with mint sprigs.

◒ medium fibre	65 calories
● low saturated fat	P:S ratio 2:1

DRIED FRUIT FEAST

The sweetness of dried fruits is a natural sweetness. Drying is an old and excellent preserving method and dried fruits are simply ripe fresh fruits that have had their moisture content drastically reduced. Because only fully ripened fruit is used, the flavour and sweetness are captured at their height, making this kind of fruit a very valuable form of concentrated goodness and nourishment. Dried fruits are also a very rich source of vitamins, minerals and important dietary fibre.

To reconstitute dried fruit, cover with cold water (or fruit juices, or cold tea) and leave to soak overnight. A quicker method is the *hot soak*; put the fruit in a saucepan, cover with cold water, bring to the boil and simmer, covered, for 10 minutes. Remove from the heat and leave to soak for 1 hour.

FRUIT MUESLI

12 SERVINGS

250 g/8 oz rolled oats
75 g/3 oz wholewheat flakes or barley flakes
25 g/1 oz whole bran-type cereal
2 tablespoons oat bran
25 g/1 oz toasted hazelnuts, skinned and chopped
75 g/3 oz sunflower seeds
300 g/10 oz dried fruit,

e.g.: 125 g/4 oz sultanas
50 g/2 oz dried apricots, chopped
125 g/4 oz dried apple rings, chopped

Mix together all the ingredients and store in an airtight container for up to 6 weeks. Serve with skimmed milk or natural yogurt.

The dried fruits can be varied according to taste. Try combinations of dried peaches, dates, figs, bananas and pears.

For added flavour lightly toast the rolled oats, oat bran and sunflower seeds until golden. Leave to cool completely before stirring into the remaining ingredients.

Remember that a bowl of crunchy muesli can be enjoyed at any hour of the day, not only at breakfast time. Top with fresh orange segments and black grapes for a quick lunch or serve with hot milk, spiced with cinnamon and a little honey, at supper time.

● high fibre	175 calories
● low saturated fat	P:S ratio 2:1

Baked fruit compote, just right for winter mornings.

HOME-MADE YOGURT

600 ml/1 pint skimmed milk
150 ml/¼ pint natural yogurt

Bring the skimmed milk to the boil. Cover and cool to 43°C/110°F (lukewarm). Whisk in the yogurt. Pour the mixture into a wide-necked 900 ml/1½ pint vacuum flask. Seal the flask and leave in a warm place for 8 to 10 hours to set.

Transfer the yogurt to a sterilized container and refrigerate. Stir in your own choice of chopped fresh or dried fruits when serving.

| ○ low fibre | 25 calories |
| ● low saturated fat | P:S ratio — |

HONEYED PORRIDGE

SERVES 4

125 g/4 oz coarse oatmeal
25 g/1 oz medium oatmeal
1.1 litres/2 pints water
1 tablespoon clear honey
4 tablespoons skimmed milk

Soak all the oatmeal in the water overnight.

Transfer the oatmeal and water to a saucepan. Bring to the boil, stirring all the time. Simmer, uncovered, for 25 minutes until the oatmeal is cooked, but still retains some bite. Stir in the honey and skimmed milk before serving.

For a delicious topping, spoon 125 g /4 oz chopped dried figs, and 1 finely chopped eating apple onto the cooked porridge.

| ◖ medium fibre | 170 calories |
| ● low saturated fat | P:S ratio 2:1 |

MUSHROOM KEDGEREE

SERVES 4

*125 g/4 oz long-grain
brown rice
250 g/8 oz smoked haddock
fillet, skinned
50 g/2 oz Flora margarine
50 g/2 oz button mushrooms,
halved
2 hard-boiled eggs, roughly
chopped
freshly ground black pepper*

Cook the rice in plenty of boiling water for about 35 minutes or until just tender. Drain well. Poach the haddock in water for 10 to 15 minutes. Drain, skin and flake.

Melt the margarine in a sauté pan. Stir in the rice, mushrooms and haddock. Cook, stirring, for 3 to 4 minutes until hot. Add the eggs and cook for a further 1 to 2 minutes. Season with pepper. Garnish with chopped fresh parsley and lemon wedges.

Crumble 2 rashers of crispy-grilled bacon over the kedgeree for added flavour.

| ◑ medium fibre | 350 calories |
| ● low saturated fat | P:S ratio 2:1 |

BREAKFAST PANCAKES

SERVES 4

*300 ml/½ pint skimmed milk
1 teaspoon fresh yeast or
½ teaspoon dried yeast
½ teaspoon soft brown sugar
125 g/4 oz plain flour
125 g/4 oz buckwheat flour
1 egg, separated
15 g/½ oz Flora margarine,
melted
a little salt
Flora Oil, to cook*

Heat the milk until just warm. Stir in the yeast. Leave for 10 to 15 minutes until frothy.

Place the sugar and flours in a bowl and gradually beat in the milk mixture. Cover and leave for about 30 minutes or until doubled in size.

Beat in the egg yolk, margarine and a little salt. Whisk the egg white until stiff and fold into the batter.

Lightly oil a non-stick frying pan. Cook small spoonfuls of batter over a moderate heat for about 2 minutes on each side or until golden. Keep warm in a low oven between layers of greaseproof paper.

Serve with Mushroom Kedgeree (see above) or Citrus Spread (see opposite).

Breakfast Pancakes can also be spread with polyunsaturated margarine and served with lightly scrambled or poached eggs as an unusual alternative to toast.

| ● high fibre | 270 calories |
| ● low saturated fat | P:S ratio 2:1 |

Perfect for brunch: Breakfast pancakes and Oat muffins served with tangy Citrus spread.

CHICKEN LIVER TOASTS

SERVES 4

50 g/2 oz Flora margarine
250 g/8 oz chicken livers,
halved and trimmed
6 tablespoons tomato juice
1 teaspoon English
mustard powder
1 teaspoon Worcestershire
sauce
a little salt
freshly ground black pepper

Melt the margarine in a small sauté pan. Over a high heat brown the livers well, a few at a time. Remove with a slotted spoon. Return all the livers to the pan with the tomato juice, mustard powder and Worcestershire sauce. Bring to the boil, stirring all the time. Cook for 1 to 2 minutes. Season with a little salt and pepper. Serve immediately on thick slices of wholemeal toast.

◑ medium fibre   190 calories
◑ med. saturated fat   P:S ratio 2:1

OAT MUFFINS

MAKES 12

4 tablespoons Flora Oil
125 g/4 oz plain wholemeal
flour
2 teaspoons baking powder
75 g/3 oz medium oatmeal
1 tablespoon wheatgerm
40 g/1½ oz soft brown sugar
1 egg
300 ml/½ pint skimmed milk

Lightly brush 12 deep bun tins with a little of the oil. Place all the dry ingredients in a bowl. Whisk together the egg, milk and remaining oil. Add to the dry ingredients and mix until just combined – don't over beat.
   Divide the mixture between the bun tins and bake in a preheated oven (200°C/400°F, Gas Mark 6) for 25 to 30 minutes.

● high fibre   450 calories
● low saturated fat   P:S ratio 3:1

CITRUS SPREAD

MAKES 250 g/8 oz

125 g/4 oz Flora margarine
125 g/4 oz low-fat soft cheese,
such as natural quark
grated rind of 1 lemon
grated rind of 1 grapefruit
pinch soft brown sugar

Beat together all the ingredients until very smooth. Spoon into a small serving dish. Cover and chill for at least 20 minutes.
   Serve this light, fluffy spread with Breakfast Pancakes (see left), or Oat Muffins (see above).

   Try beating a little honey instead of sugar into the margarine.

◑ medium fibre   135 calories
◑ med. saturated fat   P:S ratio 3:1

CAESAR SALAD

SERVES 4

75 g/3 oz sliced whole-
meal bread
1 Cos lettuce
4 eggs
8 anchovy fillets, drained and
halved lengthways
grated rind and juice of 1 lemon
4 tablespoons Flora Oil
1 clove garlic, crushed
25 g/1 oz grated Parmesan
cheese

Remove the crusts from the bread. Cut into 2.5 cm/1 inch squares. Bake in a preheated oven (200°C/400°F, Gas Mark 6) for 15 to 20 minutes or until golden and crisp.

Wash and dry the lettuce. Tear into bite-size pieces. Hard-boil 3 of the eggs. Cool, shell and quarter. Place the lettuce, bread croûtons, and eggs on a serving platter. Arrange the anchovies in a lattice over the eggs.

Boil the remaining egg for 1 minute only, then break into a bowl. Whisk in the grated lemon rind and 3 tablespoons of juice, the oil, garlic and all but 1 teaspoon of Parmesan cheese. Spoon evenly over the salad. Sprinkle with the remaining Parmesan cheese and serve immediately.

Caesar salad, a classic combination of ingredients which can be served as a starter.

◐ medium fibre		330 calories
◐ med. saturated fat		P:S ratio 2:1

TOMATO and KIDNEY SOUP

SERVES 4

25 g/1 oz Flora margarine
1 tablespoon Flora Oil
250 g/8 oz lambs' kidneys,
skinned, cored and
roughly chopped
1 clove garlic, crushed
1 teaspoon tomato paste
1 tablespoon plain flour
1.1 litres/2 pints beef stock
grated rind and juice
of 2 oranges
175 g/6 oz dried wholewheat
pasta bows, or shells
500 g/1 lb tomatoes, skinned
¼ teaspoon dried tarragon
2 tablespoons chopped
fresh parsley
a little salt
freshly ground black pepper

Heat the margarine and oil in a large saucepan and brown the kidneys well, a few at a time. Return all the kidneys to the saucepan with the garlic and tomato paste. Cook, stirring, for 1 minute before adding the flour. Cook for a further minute before adding the stock, orange rind, 8 tablespoons of orange juice and the pasta.

Bring to the boil, cover and simmer gently for 15 to 20 minutes or until the pasta is cooked.

Halve, seed and roughly chop the tomatoes. Stir into the soup with the tarragon and parsley. Season with a little salt and pepper. Simmer for 1 to 2 minutes before serving with crusty French bread or warm wholemeal rolls.

● high fibre		370 calories
● low saturated fat		P:S ratio 3:1

CHICKEN BROTH

SERVES 4

2 chicken quarters, about 700 g/
1½ lb total weight, skinned
a little salt
freshly ground black pepper
slices of carrot, onion, 4 black
peppercorns, and 1 bayleaf for
flavouring
1.1 litres/2 pints cold water
125 g/4 oz pearl barley
3 tablespoons chopped
fresh parsley
1 teaspoon chopped
fresh thyme
3 tablespoons cornflour
pinch ground turmeric
150 ml/¼ pint natural yogurt

Place the chicken quarters in a large saucepan with a little salt and pepper, the carrot, onion, peppercorns, bayleaf and cold water. Bring to the boil. Cover and simmer gently for about 45 minutes, or until the chicken is cooked (test with a skewer after 40 minutes). Remove the chicken and cool. Strain and reserve the chicken stock.

Cook the pearl barley in boiling water for about 1 hour, or until just tender. Drain well. Remove all the chicken flesh from the quarters and cut into bite-size pieces. Skim any fat from the surface of the reserved stock. Place in a saucepan with 1.3 litres/2¼ pints skimmed, reserved stock, the barley, parsley and thyme.

Mix the cornflour and turmeric to a smooth paste with 6 tablespoons water. Stir into the chicken mixture. Bring to the boil and simmer for 10 minutes stirring all the time. Off the heat, whisk in the yogurt. Season lightly with a little salt and pepper.

Reheat gently without boiling. Garnish with extra chopped fresh parsley.

This is a hearty soup with year-round potential. Serve it for lunch or supper with warm bread rolls and a green salad.

When time is at a premium use 375 g/ 12 oz of cooked, skinned chicken cut into bite-size pieces and 250 g/8 oz cooked long-grain rice with light vegetable stock.

If fresh coriander is available substitute 4 finely chopped tablespoons of the aromatic herb and omit the parsley and thyme. Its subtle flavour is excellent with chicken and yogurt.

◐ medium fibre	230 calories	
● low saturated fat	P:S ratio 0.4:1	

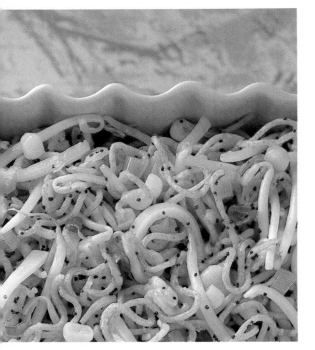

CHEESY CORN SALAD

SERVES 4

250 g/8 oz Edam cheese
3 tablespoons Flora Oil
2 tablespoons white
wine vinegar
freshly ground black pepper
2 tablespoons poppyseeds
125 g/4 oz dried spinach, egg or
wholewheat noodles
250 g/8 oz beansprouts
198 g/7 oz can sweetcorn
kernels, drained

Cut the cheese into thin matchstick-size pieces. Whisk together the oil, vinegar, pepper and poppyseeds.

Cook the noodles in boiling water for 12 to 15 minutes or until just tender. Drain well. While still hot toss in the cheese, beansprouts, sweetcorn and poppyseed dressing. Garnish with spring onion curls and serve immediately with sesame bread sticks.

This cheese and noodle salad with its poppyseed dressing is a complete meal. As a variation, omit the Edam cheese and stir in cubes of Feta cheese, or bite-size pieces of cooked chicken or lean ham.

Try using a colourful mixture of pasta such as egg with spinach.

Cheesy corn salad, best served warm with crunchy, sesame bread sticks or pitta bread.

● high fibre	457 calories	
◐ med. saturated fat	P:S ratio 0.6:1	

21

CHICKEN LIVER BOLOGNESE

SERVES 4

50 g/2 oz Flora margarine
250 g/8 oz onion,
finely chopped
125 g/4 oz carrot,
finely chopped
175 g/6 oz celery,
finely chopped
50 g/2 oz lean back bacon,
trimmed and chopped
500 g/1 lb chicken livers,
trimmed and chopped
3 tablespoons tomato paste
150 ml/1/4 pint dry red wine
150 ml/1/4 pint beef stock
1/2 teaspoon mixed dried herbs
2 bayleaves
a little salt
freshly ground black pepper
350 g/12 oz dried spaghetti

Melt the margarine in a large saucepan. Sauté the onion, carrot and celery for 3 to 4 minutes until golden. Add the bacon and chicken livers and fry until well browned.

Stir in the tomato paste, red wine and stock. Add the herbs, bayleaves and a little salt and pepper. Bring to the boil and simmer, covered, for 20 minutes.

Cook the spaghetti in boiling water for 12 to 15 minutes or until tender. Drain well. Season with plenty of black pepper. Serve with the chicken liver sauce.

To add extra flavour to the cooked spaghetti, beat together 50 g/2 oz Flora margarine, 1/2 teaspoon ground black pepper and 1 tablespoon grated Parmesan cheese. Toss into the hot pasta before serving.

| ● high fibre | 680 calories |
| ● low saturated fat | P:S ratio 2:1 |

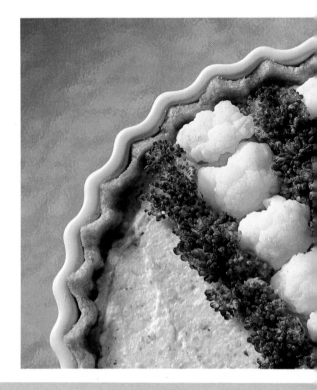

KITCHEN EXTRAS

Invest in a vegetable brush. More fibre is retained in potatoes, carrots, etc., if they are scrubbed rather than peeled. If you do peel, use a proper swivel peeler so that only a very thin layer is removed.

Choose kitchen knives carefully as they are going to be in constant use. An 18 cm/ 7 inch chef's knife is a good all-purpose knife. A small serrated one is ideal for citrus fruit and tomatoes. It pays to look after your kitchen knives. Clean, sharp knives will make chopping and trimming less of a chore.

A pressure cooker is an excellent extra to have in the kitchen. It is ideal for quick, warming soups when the weather turns chilly and speeds up the cooking of casseroles and stews. It also saves time when cooking beans and grains (see page 30).

DEVILLED TURKEY FILLETS

SERVES 4

4 turkey breast fillets, skinned
or 4 chicken thighs, skinned
and boned
3 tablespoons natural yogurt
2 tablespoons ground paprika
2 teaspoons mild
chilli seasoning
25 g/1 oz Flora margarine,
melted
1 clove garlic, crushed
a little salt
freshly ground black pepper
grated rind and juice of
1 large orange

With a sharp knife, mark a lattice of cuts across the surface of each turkey fillet. Beat together the yogurt, paprika, chilli seasoning, margarine, garlic and a little salt and pepper. Stir in the orange rind and 3 tablespoons of juice. Place the turkey in a shallow, flameproof dish. Spoon over the yogurt mixture. Cover and refrigerate for at least 1 hour or preferably overnight.

Cook the turkey under a preheated grill for about 5 minutes each side, basting with the marinade as it cooks. (Allow 7 to 8 minutes if using chicken thighs.)

Serve in warm pitta bread with a salad of shredded lettuce, thinly sliced onion and cucumber.

| ○ low fibre | 215 calories |
| ● low saturated fat | P:S ratio 2:1 |

CREAMED SPINACH CROÛTES

SERVES 4

*250 g/8 oz fresh spinach,
washed
4 eggs
125 g/4 oz Flora margarine
2 tablespoons plain flour
300 ml/½ pint skimmed milk
a little salt
freshly ground black pepper
grated nutmeg
1 clove garlic, crushed
four 2.5cm/1 inch thick slices
wholemeal bread*

Cook the spinach in a covered saucepan with no extra liquid for 3 to 4 minutes. Drain well then finely chop. Put the eggs on to poach lightly.

Melt 25 g/1 oz of the margarine in a small saucepan. Stir in the flour. Cook, stirring, for 1 minute before adding the milk. Bring to the boil and simmer for 1 to 2 minutes. Stir in the spinach, a little salt, pepper and nutmeg.

Beat the garlic into the remaining margarine. Toast the bread slices on one side. Spread the untoasted side with the garlic mixture. Toast again until golden.

Serve each croûte of wholemeal bread topped with a lightly poached egg. Spoon over the spinach sauce to completely coat the egg and serve immediately with a tomato and onion salad.

Soft cheese tart; crisp vegetables and a creamy filling inside a light wholemeal case.

● high fibre	560 calories
● low saturated fat	P : S ratio 3 : 1

SOFT CHEESE TART

SERVES 4 TO 6

PASTRY
*50 g/2 oz Flora margarine
25 g/1 oz White Flora
2 to 3 tablespoons water
75 g/3 oz plain wholemeal flour
75 g/3 oz plain flour*

FILLING
*175 g/6 oz broccoli florets,
trimmed
175 g/6 oz cauliflower
florets, trimmed
1 bunch spring onions,
finely chopped
2 rashers back bacon, trimmed
and grilled until crisp
200 g/7 oz low-fat soft cheese
2 tablespoons French Dressing
(see page 77)*

Place the margarine, white fat, water and 2 tablespoons of the wholemeal flour in a bowl and mix together well using a fork. Stir in the remaining flours and mix to a firm dough. (Add a little more water if necessary.) Turn out onto a lightly floured surface and knead until smooth.

Roll out the pastry to a round large enough to line a 20 cm/8 inch flan dish. Ease the pastry into the base and up the sides. Trim off the excess pastry with a knife and prick the base with a fork.

Line the pastry with greaseproof paper and fill with baking beans. Place in a preheated oven (200°C/400°F, Gas Mark 6) for 25 minutes or until completely cooked. Uncover for the last 5 minutes of cooking time.

Roughly chop the broccoli and cauliflower stalks. Cook the broccoli and cauliflower heads in boiling water for 10 to 12 minutes, or until just cooked. Drain well and cool.

Cook the stalks in boiling water for 15 to 20 minutes or until very tender. Drain well.

Purée together the spring onions, vegetable stalks, bacon and cheese in a blender or processor.

Spoon the purée into the pastry case. Neatly arrange the broccoli and cauliflower heads over the mixture. Spoon over the French Dressing. Garnish with sprigs of watercress.

This delicious, brightly-coloured tart is best served soon after it is assembled.

● high fibre	350 calories
● low saturated fat	P : S ratio 3 : 1

CHICKEN & LEMON RISOTTO

SERVES 4

175 g /6 oz chicken breast
fillets, skinned
75 g /3 oz onion, sliced
1 clove garlic, crushed
grated rind of 1 lemon
1 litre /1¾ pints chicken stock
250 g /8 oz long-grain
brown rice
50 g /2 oz button mushrooms
½ teaspoon ground turmeric
or paprika
a little salt
freshly ground black pepper
125 g /4 oz cooked mussels or
peeled, cooked prawns
50 g /2 oz frozen peas

Cut the chicken into bite-size pieces. Place all the ingredients except the mussels (or prawns) and peas in a large saucepan. Bring to the boil, then simmer, uncovered, for 35 to 40 minutes, stirring occasionally.

Stir in the mussels (or prawns) and peas. Continue stirring over a high heat for 4 to 5 minutes until most of the liquid has been absorbed. Spoon onto a warm serving dish and garnish with whole prawns and lemon wedges.

Crusty bread, a courgette and watercress salad tossed with Herb Dressing (see page 77) and a large platter of fresh fruit are all you need to complete this meal.

◖ medium fibre	310 calories
● low saturated fat	P:S ratio 1:1

SAFFRON SEAFOOD KEBABS

SERVES 4

500 g /1 lb monkfish or cod
fillet, skinned
125 g /4 oz cucumber
1 red pepper
1 lemon, thinly sliced
8 large cooked, shelled Pacific
prawns
4 bayleaves
75 ml /3 fl oz dry white wine
few strands saffron
pinch ground nutmeg
a little salt
freshly ground black pepper

Cut the monkfish or cod into 2.5 cm /1 inch cubes. Halve the cucumber and thickly slice. Chop the pepper into 2.5 cm /1 inch pieces.

Wrap a lemon slice around each prawn. Thread on to 4 large skewers alternately with the fish, cucumber and pepper. Finish with a bayleaf. Place in a shallow flameproof dish.

Whisk together the remaining ingredients and pour over the kebabs. Cover and marinate in the refrigerator for 1 hour.

Cook under a preheated grill for about 5 minutes on each side. Serve immediately, garnished with lemon and cucumber slices and bayleaves.

These splendid kebabs make excellent eating served straight from the grill into hot, split pitta bread with a shredded green salad.

○ low fibre	130 calories
● low saturated fat	P:S ratio 2:1

HOT TUNA MUSHROOMS

SERVES 4
---

700 g /1½ lb button mushrooms
grated rind and juice of
½ lemon
1 tablespoon chopped
fresh thyme
pinch ground coriander
a little salt
freshly ground black pepper
198 g /7 oz can tuna fish in
brine, drained

Wipe the mushrooms and cut any large ones in half. Mix together all the ingredients except the tuna fish. Transfer to a lightly greased shallow ovenproof dish. Cover tightly with foil.

Bake in a preheated oven (190°C/375°F, Gas Mark 5) for about 30 minutes. Stir in the tuna fish, cover and return to the oven for a further 10 minutes.

Hot Tuna Mushrooms makes a tasty filling for jacket-baked potatoes. Cook alongside the potatoes for the last 40 minutes of cooking time.

175 g/6 oz peeled, cooked prawns would make an excellent alternative to tuna fish.

| ● high fibre | 165 calories |
| ⊖ med. saturated fat | P:S ratio 2:1 |

Chicken & lemon risotto and Quick-fried liver, two easy meals for lunch or supper.

QUICK-FRIED LIVER

SERVES 4
---

250 g/8 oz lambs' liver
2 tablespoons Flora Oil
4 rashers lean back bacon,
trimmed and chopped
250 g/8 oz onion, thinly sliced
75 g/3 oz green pepper,
seeded and sliced
125 g/4 oz button mushrooms
400 g/14 oz can red kidney
beans, drained, or 125 g/4 oz
dried beans, soaked and cooked
(see page 30)
300 ml/½ pint chicken stock
2 tablespoons dry sherry
4 tablespoons chopped
fresh parsley

Slice the liver into thin, finger-length strips.

Heat the oil in a medium sauté pan or wok and fry the bacon, onion and pepper until golden. Remove with a slotted spoon. Drain on absorbent kitchen paper.

Add the liver and sliced mushrooms to the pan and cook over a high heat, stirring all the time, until well browned. Return the bacon mixture to the pan, add the beans and stir over the heat for a further 2 minutes.

Add the stock, sherry and pepper. Cook uncovered for 5 minutes, until much of the liquid has evaporated. Sprinkle with the chopped parsley, garnish with bayleaves and serve immediately.

An excellent method of cooking liver to ensure it is moist and flavourful every time.

| ● high fibre | 280 calories |
| ⊖ med. saturated fat | P:S ratio 0.9:1 |

MONDAY'S PIE

SERVES 4

700 g /1½ lb potatoes, peeled
125 g /4 oz onion, chopped
2 tablespoons Flora Oil
2 tablespoons plain flour
300 ml /½ pint beef or
chicken stock
500 g /1 lb cooked beef, lamb or
chicken, trimmed of fat and
coarsely minced
1 tablespoon Worcestershire
sauce
4 tablespoons chopped
fresh parsley
a little salt
freshly ground black pepper
2 eggs, separated

Cook the potatoes in boiling water, until tender. Sauté the onion in the oil until well browned. Stir in the flour. Cook for 1 to 2 minutes before adding the stock. Bring to the boil and simmer gently until thickened.

Stir in the minced meat, Worcestershire sauce, parsley, and a little salt and pepper. Spoon into a 1.1 litre /2 pint shallow pie dish.

Drain the potatoes. Mash or sieve until smooth then beat in the egg yolks and a little salt and pepper. Stiffly whisk the egg whites and fold into the potato mixture. Spoon evenly over the meat mixture.

Bake in a preheated oven (200°C/400°F, Gas Mark 6) for 30 to 40 minutes or until well browned. Serve with parsleyed carrots or parsnips.

◑ medium fibre	515 calories
◑ med. saturated fat	P:S ratio 0.7:1

EASTERN PEPPERS

SERVES 4

4 mixed peppers
(yellow, red, green)
2 tablespoons Flora Oil
250 g/8 oz onion, chopped
1 clove garlic, crushed
1 tablespoon chopped
fresh mint
¼ teaspoon ground cinnamon
¼ teaspoon ground paprika
500 g/1 lb lean minced beef, or
leg of lamb
175 g/6 oz tomatoes, skinned
and chopped
175 g/6 oz long-grain white rice
125 g/4 oz raisins
6 tablespoons beef stock
50 g/2 oz walnut pieces,
chopped
600 ml/1 pint water

Cut a thin slice from the stalk end of each pepper and reserve. Remove the seeds. Place side by side in a shallow, ovenproof dish.

Heat the oil in a saucepan and sauté the onion with the garlic, mint, cinnamon and paprika for 3 to 4 minutes. Add the minced beef or lamb and cook, stirring, over a high heat until lightly browned. Carefully pour off the excess fat. Stir in the remaining ingredients, bring to the boil and simmer for 10 minutes until the rice is half-cooked and the liquids almost absorbed.

Fill the peppers with the meat and rice mixture. Replace the reserved tops. Cover the dish loosely with foil.

Bake in a preheated oven (190°C/375°F, Gas Mark 5) for about 40 minutes. Serve immediately.

The simple pepper treated with a little imagination can be transformed into a delicious supper dish. Here it is filled with a light meat and tomato mixture. The filling gains added flavour from mint, cinnamon and paprika; an unusual combination which produces delicious results.

These peppers are also good with other herbs such as parsley and coriander instead of spices.

● high fibre	465 calories
◑ med. saturated fat	P:S ratio 0.8:1

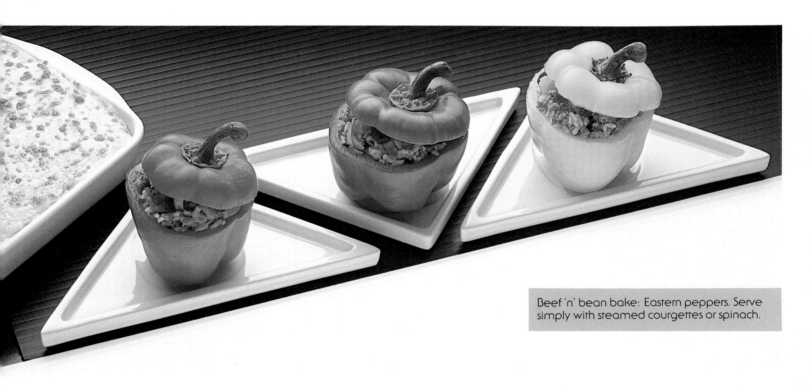

Beef 'n' bean bake: Eastern peppers. Serve simply with steamed courgettes or spinach.

BEEF 'N' BEAN BAKE

SERVES 4

75 g/3 oz Flora margarine
50 g/2 oz onion, chopped
250 g/8 oz lean, minced beef
65 g/2½ oz plain flour
200 ml/7 fl oz beef stock
freshly ground black pepper
250 g/8 oz tomatoes, skinned
and chopped
400 g/14 oz can butter beans, or
125 g/4 oz dried beans soaked
and cooked (see page 30)
1 tablespoon tomato paste
¼ teaspoon dried oregano
¼ teaspoon dried basil
pinch of English
mustard powder
300 ml/½ pint skimmed milk
50 g/2 oz Mozzarella
cheese, grated

Melt 25 g/1 oz of the margarine in a medium saucepan. Stir in the onion and sauté for 3 to 4 minutes until golden. Add the minced beef and cook, stirring over a high heat for 3 to 4 minutes. Carefully pour off any excess fat. Stir in 40 g/1½ oz of the flour, the stock, and pepper. Bring to the boil and cook, uncovered, for 2 to 3 minutes. Place in a deep, 1.7 litre/3 pint ovenproof dish.

Melt 25 g/1 oz margarine in the saucepan. Add the tomatoes, drained beans, tomato paste and herbs. Simmer, uncovered, for 2 to 3 minutes or until quite thick. Spoon over the meat mixture.

Melt the remaining margarine in a saucepan. Stir in the remaining flour and mustard powder. Cook, stirring, for 1 to 2 minutes before adding the milk. Bring to the boil and simmer until thickened. Off the heat beat in half the cheese and pour over the bean mixture. Sprinkle with the remaining cheese.

Bake in a preheated oven (200°C/400°F, Gas Mark 6) for about 25 to 30 minutes or until golden brown. Serve hot.

Whether you're a busy cook who likes to freeze ahead for future meals, or someone with a hungry family to satisfy, this bake is the answer.

Any canned or dried beans can be used if butter beans are not available. Try red kidney, cannellini or flageolet.

| ● high fibre | 460 calories |
| ◒ med. saturated fat | P:S ratio 2:1 |

WINTER BEEF CASSEROLE

SERVES 4

1 tablespoon Flora Oil
2 leeks, sliced
4 carrots, sliced
1 kohlrabi, peeled and chopped
or 350 g/12 oz turnip
125 g/4 oz button mushrooms,
sliced
500 g/1 lb lean braising steak,
trimmed and cut into strips
125 g/4 oz pearl barley
600 ml/1 pint beef stock
300 ml/½ pint stout or light ale
3 tablespoons chopped fresh
parsley or watercress
a little salt
freshly ground black pepper

Winter beef casserole, tastes even better if made the day before. Serve with parsleyed potatoes.

Heat the oil in a large frying pan. Add the leeks, carrots, kohlrabi or turnip and mushrooms. Cook for 2 to 3 minutes stirring. Using a slotted spoon place the vegetables in a casserole.

Add the meat to the frying pan, fry quickly to brown evenly. Stir in the barley, stock, stout or light ale, parsley or watercress, and a little salt and pepper. Bring to the boil.

Pour the meat mixture into the casserole, and stir well. Cover and cook in a preheated oven (160°C/325°F, Gas Mark 3) for 1½ to 2 hours or until the meat is tender. Serve hot garnished with watercress sprigs.

This is the kind of rich, hearty but simple food that is equally appropriate for family or friends. A dish of piping hot parsleyed potatoes is the only accompaniment necessary.

| ● high fibre | 415 calories |
| ● low saturated fat | P:S ratio 0.9:1 |

SPICY CITRUS CHICKEN

SERVES 4

1 tablespoon plain flour
½ teaspoon each ground
turmeric, ground coriander,
ground cumin
freshly ground black pepper
4 chicken breast fillets
or chicken thighs, skinned
1 tablespoon Flora Oil
grated rind and juice of 1 orange
grated rind and juice of 1 lime
2 teaspoons clear honey
1 onion, finely chopped
250 g/8 oz split red lentils
600 ml/1 pint chicken stock

Place the flour, turmeric, coriander, cumin, and pepper in a polythene bag. Add the chicken and shake well to coat evenly.

Heat the oil in a frying pan, add the chicken and cook gently for 4 minutes, turning once. Stir in any remaining spice mixture, grated orange and lime rinds and juice, and the honey. Bring to the boil, cover and simmer for 15 minutes, or until tender. Test with a skewer. The juices should run clear.

Meanwhile place the onion, lentils and stock in a saucepan, bring to the boil, cover and cook very gently for about 25 minutes until all the stock has been absorbed. Arrange the lentils around the edge of a warmed serving dish or individual plates.

Place the chicken in the centre and pour the sauce over. Garnish with coriander or bayleaves, orange and lime twists.

The distinctive tang of orange and lime, combined with subtle spices, turns this into a very special main course.

Red lentils provide a delicious and colourful accompaniment. For a simple alternative serve brown rice or pasta noodles tossed with chopped spring onions.

Chicken legs or turkey breast fillets can also be 'spiced' in this way. Allow an extra 5 to 10 minutes' cooking time if using chicken legs.

| ● high fibre | 350 calories |
| ● low saturated fat | P:S ratio 1.5:1 |

CHICKEN and BACON PIE

SERVES 6 TO 8

FILLING
3 chicken breast fillets, skinned
and thinly sliced
50 g/2 oz lean back bacon,
trimmed and chopped
125 g/4 oz mushrooms, sliced
1 tablespoon chopped
fresh tarragon
grated rind and juice of
1 lemon
freshly ground black pepper

PASTRY
275 g/10 oz plain flour
50 g/2 oz Flora margarine
75 g/3 oz White Flora
3 tablespoons cold water, to mix
beaten egg or milk, to glaze

Mix together in a bowl the chicken, bacon, mushrooms, tarragon, lemon rind and juice and some black pepper.

Place the flour in a bowl, add the margarine and white fat and rub in until the mixture resembles fine breadcrumbs. Stir in the water and mix with a fork to a firm dough. Turn out onto a floured surface and knead lightly.

Roll out half of the pastry to a round large enough to line the base of a 20 cm/8 inch ovenproof pie plate.

Spread the chicken and bacon filling evenly over the pastry base.

Roll out the remaining pastry to a round large enough to cover the filling. Dampen the pastry edge with water and place lid in position. Press the edges together firmly to seal and carefully trim off any excess pastry with a sharp knife.

Flute the pastry edge and make a hole in the centre. Finish the pie with pastry leaves made from the trimmings and brush with beaten egg or milk.

Place the pie in a preheated oven (180°C/350°F, Gas Mark 4) for 40 to 45 minutes until the pastry is golden. Serve hot or cold.

The chicken breast fillets are quick and easy to use but you may substitute half a small chicken, skinned, boned and sliced or 3 chicken legs, skinned, boned and sliced.

Tarragon is particularly good with chicken and mushrooms but any fresh or dried herbs may be used.

◖ medium fibre	295 calories
● low saturated fat	P:S ratio 2:1

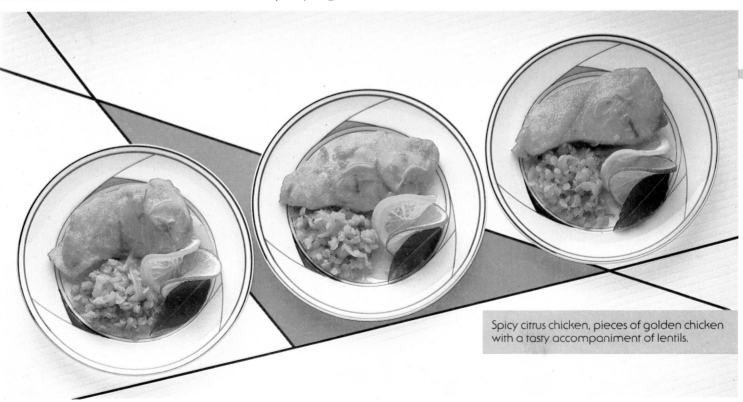

Spicy citrus chicken, pieces of golden chicken with a tasty accompaniment of lentils.

RABBIT BEAN POT

SERVES 4

*75 g/3 oz dried red kidney
beans, soaked overnight
(see page 30)
75 g/3 oz dried cannellini
beans, soaked overnight
(see page 30)
1 tablespoon Flora Oil
2 leeks, sliced
4 carrots, sliced
4 rabbit joints, skinned
600 ml/1 pint chicken stock
a little salt
freshly ground black pepper
1 tablespoon cornflour
1 tablespoon cold water
2 tablespoons chopped fresh
parsley or coriander*

Rinse the beans in fresh water, place in a saucepan and cover with cold water. Bring to the boil and cook rapidly for 10 minutes, then drain.

Heat the oil in a large frying pan, add the leeks and carrots and cook for 2 to 3 minutes. Using a slotted spoon, place the vegetables in a flameproof casserole.

Add the rabbit joints to the frying pan and cook quickly to brown on all sides. Drain on absorbent kitchen paper. Arrange the rabbit on top of the vegetables.

Pour the stock into the frying pan, add the beans, bring to the boil, and add a little salt and pepper. Transfer the stock and beans to the casserole, cover and cook in a preheated oven (160°C/325°F, Gas Mark 3) for 2 hours or until the rabbit and beans are tender.

Blend the cornflour and water together to a smooth paste, then stir into the casserole. Bring to the boil. Simmer until thickened. Sprinkle with chopped parsley or coriander and serve hot.

Rabbit can often be a little bland but not when it is prepared using this method, which can be applied equally successfully to pheasant, or chicken.

This is an adaptable recipe suited to all kinds of beans and vegetables; there are many delicious changes that can be made. Try using butter beans and chick peas with onion and parsnips or red kidney and flageolet beans with leeks and turnips.

● high fibre	370 calories
● low saturated fat	P:S ratio 1:1

BEAN CUISINE

Dried peas, beans and lentils, known as pulses, are cheap, readily available and store well. Lentils and split peas can be cooked straight away, but beans and whole peas should be soaked before cooking. To do this, simply put them into a deep bowl and cover with their height again in cold water. Leave for 6 to 8 hours. Alternatively, boil the pulses for 2 minutes, cover and leave to soak in the water for 1 hour. Whichever method you use, drain and rinse the pulses after soaking, cover them with fresh, cold water and boil rapidly for 10 minutes. Let the pulses simmer gently until they're tender, usually about 45 minutes to 1 hour (25 to 30 minutes for lentils), and use as required.
125 g/4 oz of dried beans, soaked and cooked, corresponds to a 400 g/14 oz can of beans.

COUNTRY MEAT LOAF

SERVES 6 TO 8

*250 g/8 oz boneless rabbit,
minced
250 g/8 oz lean chuck
steak, minced
250 g/8 oz boned chicken flesh,
skinned and minced
125 g/4 oz button mushrooms,
minced
1 onion, minced
50 g/2 oz jumbo oats
50 g/2 oz bran flakes
150 ml/1/4 pint chicken stock
2 tablespoons chopped
fresh parsley
1 egg, beaten
a little salt
freshly ground black pepper
Flora Oil*

Place all the ingredients except the oil in a large mixing bowl. Mix together until evenly blended.

Lightly oil a 1 kg/2 lb loaf tin and place the mixture in the tin. Level the top and cover with a piece of foil. Place in a preheated oven (180°C/350°F, Gas Mark 4) for 1 hour.

Remove the foil and leave the meat loaf in the tin for 5 minutes before inverting onto a serving plate. Garnish with sliced mushrooms, tomato wedges and parsley.

Satisfying enough to serve as a main course, delicious enough cold to have in a salad. Country Meat Loaf is so simple to assemble that you will make it often.

● high fibre	400 calories
● low saturated fat	P:S ratio 1:1

PILAFF of PORK

SERVES 4

MARINADE
4 tablespoons natural yogurt
2 teaspoons clear honey
grated rind and juice of 1 lime
2 fresh bayleaves

PILAFF
350 g/12 oz pork tenderloin,
trimmed and sliced
175 g/6 oz bulgar wheat
1 tablespoon Flora margarine
3 spring onions, chopped
125 g/4 oz mushrooms, sliced
600 ml/1 pint chicken stock
125 g/4 oz shelled broad beans
125 g/4 oz bobby beans, sliced
1 yellow pepper, seeded
and chopped
a little salt
freshly ground black pepper
fresh bayleaves

Mix together in a bowl the yogurt, honey, lime rind and juice and bayleaves. Add the pork and stir to coat evenly. Cover the bowl with cling film and leave overnight in a cool place.

Place the bulgar wheat on a piece of foil in a grill pan and toast under a moderate heat until golden brown.

Melt the margarine in a saucepan, add the onions and mushrooms and cook for 2 minutes until tender. Stir in the wheat and stock, bring to the boil, cover and cook very gently for about 10 minutes or until all the stock has been absorbed. Keep warm.

Cook the beans and pepper in boiling water for 2 to 3 minutes until almost tender. Drain and add to the bulgar wheat mixture, stirring well until evenly mixed. Season with a little salt and pepper.

Place the pork in a grill pan and cook under a moderate heat for 6 to 8 minutes, turning once.

Arrange the bulgar wheat pilaff on a warmed serving dish with the pork and garnish with fresh bayleaves.

Apart from considerable savings on housekeeping bills, meals made with grains offer extra variety in taste and texture. Bulgar wheat is one of the quickest cooking grains and makes a refreshing change from rice in this elegant, light and tasty dish.

If fresh limes are unavailable use 1 small orange or 1 lemon. Other vegetables can easily be substituted for the ones used here. Try sliced French beans, courgettes and leeks.

● high fibre	365 calories
● low saturated fat	P:S ratio 1:1

WEST COUNTRY COBBLER

SERVES 4

1 tablespoon Flora Oil
500 g/1 lb lean pork tenderloin,
thinly sliced
1 onion, sliced
1 cooking apple, peeled, cored
and chopped
4 tomatoes, skinned and
chopped
150 ml/¼ pint pure
unsweetened apple juice
a little salt
freshly ground black pepper

TOPPING
250 g/8 oz self-raising white or
wholemeal flour
50 g/2 oz Flora margarine
½ teaspoon dried sage
150 ml/¼ pint natural yogurt

Heat the oil in a frying pan, add the pork and fry quickly until evenly coloured. Using a slotted spoon place the pork in a shallow ovenproof dish.

Add the onions and apple to the frying pan and cook for 2 minutes, then stir in the tomatoes, apple juice, and a little salt and pepper. Bring to the boil and pour evenly over the pork.

Place the flour in a bowl, add the margarine and rub in finely until the mixture resembles breadcrumbs. Stir in the sage and yogurt with a fork and mix lightly until the mixture forms a soft dough. Turn out on a floured surface and knead very lightly. Don't overwork or the topping will be tough.

Roll out the dough to 1cm/½ inch thickness and cut out fifteen 5 cm/2 inch rounds with a plain cutter.

Arrange the scone rounds in an even overlapping circle around the edge of the dish. Place in a preheated oven (200°C/400°F, Gas Mark 6) for 20 minutes or until the scones are well risen, golden brown, and just firm to the touch.

Such a flavoursome dish should be served with nothing but a simple green vegetable such as Braised Celery (see page 67).

For a quick, crunchy top make the topping for Oaty Lamb (see page 32) and spread evenly over the surface of the meat mixture. Bake as above for 25 to 30 minutes.

● high fibre	585 calories
● low saturated fat	P:S ratio 1:1

Turkey loaf, a stunning mix of fresh and dried fruit, tender turkey and crisp pastry.

TURKEY LOAF

SERVES 6

three 250 g/8 oz turkey
fillets, skinned

STUFFING
1 small onion, finely chopped
2 tablespoons finely chopped
cooking apple
75 g/3 oz dried apricots,
chopped
2 teaspoons Flora margarine
25 g/1 oz fresh wholemeal
breadcrumbs
2 teaspoons chopped
fresh thyme
freshly ground black pepper
Flora Oil
125 g/4 oz Wholemeal pastry
(see page 76)
beaten egg, to glaze

OATY LAMB

SERVES 4

1 teaspoon Flora margarine
1 onion, finely chopped
1 tablespoon plain flour
500 g/1 lb cooked,
minced lamb
1 tablespoon light soy sauce
150 ml/¼ pint beef stock
1 tablespoon tomato paste
a little salt
freshly ground black pepper

TOPPING
125 g/4 oz plain or wholemeal
flour
50 g/2 oz Flora margarine
50 g/2 oz jumbo oats
1 tablespoon sesame seeds

Place the turkey fillets between two pieces of cling film and bat out with a rolling pin.

Sauté the onion, apple and apricots in the margarine for 2 minutes. Stir in the breadcrumbs, thyme, and pepper.

Brush the base of a roasting tin with a little oil and lay one turkey fillet in it. Spread the fillet with half of the stuffing, then place another turkey fillet on top. Cover with the remaining stuffing and turkey fillet.

Roll the pastry out thinly and cut out narrow strips. Arrange the strips in a lattice over the turkey fillets and trim to fit.

Brush all over with beaten egg to glaze and place in a preheated oven (190°C/375°F Gas Mark 5) for 45 minutes or until golden.

Garnish with apricot and apple slices, and sprigs of dill or chervil. Serve hot or cold.

- ● high fibre — 235 calories
- ● low saturated fat — P:S ratio 3:1

VEGETABLE CURRY

SERVES 4 TO 6

750 ml/1 1/4 pint light stock
125 g/4 oz carrots, chopped
125 g/4 oz turnips, chopped
125 g/4 oz Jerusalem
artichokes, chopped (optional)
125 g/4 oz potatoes, chopped
125 g/4 oz cauliflower florets
4 sticks celery, sliced
2 onions, sliced
1 tablespoon Flora Oil
2 tablespoons plain flour
2 tablespoons garam masala
6 green cardamom pods
1 tablespoon peeled and grated
fresh root ginger
grated rind and juice of 1 lemon
400 g/14 oz can chick peas,
drained or 125 g/4 oz dried
chick peas, soaked and cooked
(see page 30)

Place the stock in a large saucepan, bring to the boil and add the carrots, turnips, artichokes (if using), potatoes, cauliflower, celery and onions. Cook gently for 2 to 3 minutes until almost tender. Strain, reserving the stock.

Make the sauce. Heat the oil in a saucepan. Stir in all the remaining ingredients except the chick peas. Cook, stirring for 1 to 2 minutes before adding the reserved stock. Bring to the boil, cover and cook gently for 30 minutes.

Add all the vegetables and chick peas and stir over a moderate heat until the vegetables are hot, about 3 to 4 minutes. Serve the vegetable curry with cooked rice and Raita (natural yogurt and diced cucumber).

- ● high fibre — 200 calories
- ● low saturated fat — P:S ratio 4:1

Heat the margarine in a saucepan, add the onion and cook for 2 minutes until tender. Stir in the flour, lamb, soy sauce, stock, tomato paste and a little salt and pepper. Bring to the boil, stirring, and cook for 1 minute. Pour the lamb mixture into a shallow ovenproof dish.

Place the flour in a bowl, add the margarine and rub in finely until the mixture resembles breadcrumbs. Stir in the oats and sesame seeds until well mixed.

Spread the crumble topping evenly over the meat to cover completely. Place in a preheated oven (190°C/375°F, Gas Mark 5) for 25 to 30 minutes or until the topping is golden brown.

- ● high fibre — 460 calories
- ● low saturated fat — P:S ratio 2:1

WINTER MOUSSAKA

SERVES 4

700 g/1 1/2 lb aubergine
2 tablespoons Flora Oil
250 g/8 oz onion, chopped
124 g/4 oz mushrooms, sliced
1 clove garlic, crushed
1 tablespoon chopped
fresh parsley
550 g/1 1/4 lb tomatoes, chopped
1 tablespoon peanut butter
freshly ground black pepper
50 g/2 oz fresh wholemeal
breadcrumbs

SAUCE
25 g/1 oz Flora margarine
25 g/1 oz plain flour
300 ml/1/2 pint skimmed milk
50 g/2 oz Brie, chopped
1 egg, separated

Slice the aubergine. Blanch in boiling water for 4 minutes. Drain. Brown under a hot grill. Heat the oil and sauté the onion, mushrooms and garlic for 2 to 3 minutes. Stir in the parsley, tomatoes, peanut butter and pepper. Arrange layers of aubergine, tomato mixture and breadcrumbs in an ovenproof casserole, finishing with a layer of aubergine. Melt the margarine. Stir in the flour. Cook, stirring, for 1 to 2 minutes before adding the milk. Bring to the boil, simmer for 2 to 3 minutes. Beat in the Brie and egg yolk. Stiffly whisk the egg white and fold into the sauce. Spoon evenly over the aubergine. Bake in a preheated oven (180°C/359°F, Gas Mark 4) for 45 minutes.

- ◐ medium fibre — 345 calories
- ◐ med. saturated fat — P:S ratio 1:1

SEA BASS with STIR-FRY VEGETABLES

SERVES 4

1 kg/2 lb sea bass, cleaned
1 shallot, finely chopped
1 tablespoon chopped
fresh parsley
150 ml/¼ pint dry white wine
or cider
freshly ground black pepper
1 tablespoon Flora Oil
2 carrots, cut into strips
2 courgettes, cut into strips
1 small fennel bulb, cut into strips
125 g/4 oz button mushrooms,
thinly sliced
1 teaspoon cornflour
½ teaspoon clear honey

To serve the fish whole, remove the backbone from the fish keeping the head and tail intact. Alternatively, remove the head and tail and cut the fish into eight steaks.

Place the shallot, parsley, wine or cider, and a little salt and pepper in a shallow ovenproof dish and lay the fish on top. Cover with foil and place in a preheated oven (190°C/375°F, Gas Mark 5) for 30 to 40 minutes for whole fish and 15 to 20 minutes for steaks. Place the fish on a warmed serving dish. Cover and keep warm in a low oven. Reserve fish liquor.

Heat the oil in a large frying pan or wok. Add the carrots, courgettes, fennel and mushrooms. Cook for 2 to 3 minutes, stirring well until the vegetables are almost tender. Arrange around the fish and keep warm.

Pour the reserved fish liquor into the pan and bring to the boil. Blend the cornflour with a little cold water and stir into the fish liquor with the honey. Cook for 1 minute. Pour the sauce over the fish and garnish with the feathery fennel tops and lemon wedges.

Mackerel, red mullet or trout could also be used. Buy small fish about 250 g/8 oz each.

◑ medium fibre	440 calories
◑ med. saturated fat	P:S ratio 3:1

FISHERMAN'S PIE

SERVES 4

500 g/1 lb haddock fillet,
skinned
300 ml/½ pint skimmed milk
25 g/1 oz Flora margarine
125 g/4 oz celery, thinly sliced
25 g/1 oz plain flour
3 eggs, hard-boiled, shelled
and chopped
1 tablespoon chopped
celery tops
a little salt
freshly ground black pepper

TOPPING
500 g/1 lb potatoes, peeled and
roughly diced
1 teaspoon Flora margarine
50 g/2 oz Edam or a low-fat
Cheddar-type cheese, grated

Cut the fish into 4 pieces and place in a saucepan with the milk. Bring to the boil and cook gently for 3 to 4 minutes until the fish flakes easily. Remove using a slotted spoon and flake with a fork. Reserve the milk.

Heat the margarine in a saucepan. Stir in the celery, cook for 3 or 4 minutes. Stir in the flour. Add the milk and bring to the boil. Cook over a low heat for 2 minutes then stir in the eggs, celery tops, fish, a little salt and pepper until well mixed. Pour the mixture into four individual ovenproof dishes.

Cook the potatoes in boiling lightly salted water for 2 to 3 minutes until almost tender. Drain well then toss in the margarine.

Pile the potatoes on top of the fish mixture and sprinkle with grated cheese. Place in a preheated oven (190°C/375°F, Gas Mark 5) for 20 to 25 minutes or until golden brown.

Garnish with lemon twists and celery tops.

Sea bass with stir-fry vegetables and individual Fisherman's pies.

◑ medium fibre	142 calories
◑ med. saturated fat	P:S ratio 0.8:1

GINGERED LIME TROUT

SERVES 4

*four 250 g/8 oz rainbow trout,
cleaned
1 tablespoon peeled and freshly
grated root ginger
grated rind and juice of 1 lime
1 teaspoon clear honey
1 tablespoon chopped fresh dill
25 g/1 oz pine kernels
or 25 g/1 oz flaked almonds
a little salt
freshly ground black pepper*

Remove the heads and fins from the trout if wished. Wash well and dry on absorbent kitchen paper. Arrange the trout in a shallow ovenproof dish.

Mix together in a bowl the ginger, lime rind and juice, honey, dill, half of the pine kernels and a little salt and pepper. Spoon some of the ginger mixture into the cavity of each fish and pour the remainder around the trout; cover with foil.

Place the trout in a preheated oven (190°C/ 375°F, Gas Mark 5) for about 20 minutes or until the fish flakes easily with a knife.

Toast the remaining pine kernels under a moderate grill until golden brown. Arrange the trout on a warmed serving dish, garnish with the pine kernels, sprigs of dill, strips of ginger and lime twists.

Use a small pinch of ground ginger if the fresh root is unavailable.

| ○ low fibre | 280 calories |
| ● low saturated fat | P:S ratio 1:1 |

SESAME CHEESE ROLL

SERVES 4

250 g/8 oz low-fat soft cheese
2 tablespoons finely chopped
fresh parsley
1 tablespoon sesame seeds

SALAD DRESSING
3 tablespoons natural yogurt
1 tablespoon red wine vinegar
1 teaspoon clear honey

SALAD
125 g/4 oz long-grain white rice
a little salt
2 red-skinned apples, cored
and chopped
4 sticks celery, chopped
10 cm/4 inch piece cucumber,
chopped
8 radishes, thinly sliced

Form the cheese into a short roll about 4 cm/1½ inches across. Mix together on a plate the parsley and sesame seeds until evenly blended. Turn the cheese roll in the parsley mixture until evenly coated. Place on a plate and chill.

Place the yogurt, vinegar and honey in a bowl and stir until well blended. Cook the rice in boiling, lightly salted water for 12 to 15 minutes until the grains are tender. Drain and rinse under cold water. Add the rice, apples, celery, cucumber and radish slices to the salad dressing and stir gently to coat evenly. Spread the rice salad evenly over a small serving plate.

Place the cheese roll on the salad and cut into thick slices. Serve with fresh crusty bread or toasted wholemeal rolls.

◑ medium fibre	240 calories
● low saturated fat	P:S ratio 0.4:1

RICE PERFECTION

Brown rice, now widely available, has a chewy texture and delicious nutty flavour. There are several ways of cooking this particular grain. The most common method is to bring a saucepan of water to the boil. Add the rice and boil for 30 minutes or until the grains are tender, then drain. Alternatively, put the rice in a saucepan with double its volume in water (i.e. 1 cup of rice to 2 cups of water), bring to the boil, then cover and simmer over a very low heat for 45 minutes, when the rice should be cooked and all the water absorbed. Brown rice can be cooked in a pressure cooker. Put the rice in the pressure cooker pan using the same proportions as above. Bring up to pressure and cook for 10 minutes at high. Allow the pressure to reduce naturally. The rice should be perfectly cooked.

ITALIAN PASTA SALAD

SERVES 4

50 g/2 oz wholewheat or egg
pasta shells
50 g/2 oz spinach pasta shells
a little salt
1 red pepper, chopped
1 yellow pepper, chopped
198 g/7 oz can tuna in brine,
drained
12 black olives, stoned
75 g/3 oz mangetouts
75 g/3 oz French beans
125 g/4 oz cauliflower florets
4 tablespoons light stock
3 hard-boiled eggs, shelled

DRESSING
3 tablespoons natural yogurt
grated rind and juice of 1 orange
1 teaspoon dried basil

Cook the pasta shells in plenty of boiling salted water for 12 minutes or until tender. Drain well and rinse under cold water.

Place the pasta, peppers, tuna and olives in a bowl and mix gently together.

Cook the mangetouts, beans and cauliflower in stock for 4 to 5 minutes until almost tender. Drain well and cool. Quarter the eggs.

Mix together in a bowl the yogurt, 1 teaspoon orange rind and 3 tablespoons orange juice, and the basil. Pour the dressing over the pasta mixture and stir gently to coat evenly. Pile the salad in the centre of a serving dish.

Arrange the mangetouts, beans, cauliflower and egg quarters around the pasta salad.

● high fibre	335 calories
● low saturated fat	P:S ratio 1:1

BEAN and LEAF SALAD

SERVES 4

175 g/6 oz mixed dried beans
(e.g. kidney, black, butter,
cannellini or flageolet), soaked
overnight (see page 30)
600 ml/1 pint light stock
1 small radicchio, trimmed
1 bunch watercress, trimmed
1 head chicory, trimmed

DRESSING
2 tablespoons Flora Oil
2 tablespoons lemon juice
1 clove garlic, crushed
1 tablespoon chopped
fresh parsley
1½ teaspoons dried marjoram

Ideal for light, warm-weather
lunches: Sesame cheese roll with
rice salad; Cottage quiche.

Rinse the beans well under fresh water and
place together in a saucepan with the stock.
Bring to the boil and cook rapidly for 10
minutes. Cover the saucepan with a lid and
cook very gently for about 1½ hours or until
the beans are tender. Drain well and cool.

Separate the salad leaves, wash and drain
well. Arrange the leaves in an attractive
pattern on a round serving dish. Cover
loosely with clingfilm and refrigerate until
required.

Place the oil, lemon juice, garlic and
chopped herbs in a bowl and whisk until
well blended. Pour the dressing over the
beans, stir well to coat evenly.

Pile the beans in the centre of the salad
leaves and garnish with sliced spring onions
or chopped chives.

- high fibre   190 calories
- low saturated fat   P:S ratio 4:1

COTTAGE QUICHE

SERVES 6

PASTRY
25 g/1 oz Flora margarine
50 g/2 oz White Flora
2 to 3 tablespoons cold water
175 g/6 oz plain wholemeal
flour

FILLING
300 ml/½ pint light stock
125 g/4 oz split red lentils
250 g/8 oz courgettes,
thinly sliced
150 ml/¼ pint skimmed milk
2 eggs
125 g/4 oz low-fat cottage
cheese, sieved
a little salt
freshly ground black pepper

Place the margarine, white fat, water and 2
tablespoons of the wholemeal flour in a bowl
and mix together well using a fork. Stir in the
remaining flour and mix to a firm dough.
Turn out onto a lightly floured surface and
knead gently until smooth.

Roll out the pastry to a round large enough
to line a 22 cm/9 inch flan dish. Ease the
pastry into the base and up the sides. Trim off
the excess pastry with a knife and prick the
base with a fork.

Line the pastry with greaseproof paper and
fill with baking beans. Place in a preheated
oven (200°C/400°F, Gas Mark 6) for 10
minutes or until the pastry is just cooked.
Remove the paper and beans.

Place the stock in a saucepan, bring to the
boil, add the lentils and cook gently for
about 25 minutes or until all the stock has
been absorbed. Remove from the heat.

Cook the courgettes in boiling water until
just tender, drain well.

Place the milk and eggs in a bowl, whisk
until well blended. Stir in the cottage cheese,
a little salt, pepper and the lentils. Mix well
together and pour into the pastry case.

Scatter the courgettes evenly over the
surface of the flan and place in a preheated
oven (160°C/325°F, Gas Mark 3) for 35 to 40
minutes or until the filling is just set. Serve
hot or cold.

When fresh asparagus is in season it makes
a delicious alternative to courgettes. Cook as
for courgettes and cut into short lengths
before using.

- high fibre   320 calories
- low saturated fat   P:S ratio 2:1

ICED LIME SOUFFLE

SERVES 6

25 g/1 oz walnut pieces
25 g/1 oz granulated sugar
2 limes (or 2 small lemons)
3 eggs, separated
50 g/2 oz caster sugar
300 ml/½ pint natural yogurt
3 tablespoons single cream
1 tablespoon powdered gelatine

TO DECORATE
50 g/2 oz low-fat soft cheese
2 tablespoons natural yogurt
lime wedges

Place the walnuts and granulated sugar in a small saucepan. Heat gently, stirring occasionally until the sugar has dissolved and caramelized. Pour onto a lightly oiled baking sheet. When set, place in a polythene bag and crush with a rolling pin.

Finely grate the lime rind. Whisk with the egg yolks and caster sugar until thick.

Whisk the yogurt until smooth then fold into the egg mixture, with the crushed walnuts and cream.

Sprinkle the gelatine over 4 tablespoons of lime juice in a small bowl. Leave to soak for 3 minutes. Stand in a pan of simmering water and heat gently until dissolved. Fold into the egg mixture. Chill until beginning to set.

Whisk the egg whites and fold in. Spoon into a serving dish and freeze until firm.

To serve the soufflé: beat together the soft cheese and yogurt to a smooth piping consistency. Spoon or pipe onto the frozen soufflé. Allow the soufflé to soften slightly for 15 to 20 minutes in the refrigerator. Decorate with lime wedges before serving.

| ○ low fibre | 150 calories |
| ◐ med. saturated fat | P:S ratio 0.8:1 |

VANILLA CHEESECAKE

SERVES 6 TO 8

125 g/4 oz crunchy toasted
breakfast cereal
50 g/2 oz Flora margarine
250 g/8 oz low-fat soft cheese
4 tablespoons clear honey
few drops of vanilla essence
300 ml/½ pint natural yogurt
grated rind and juice of 1 lemon
1½ tablespoons powdered
gelatine
3 tablespoons water
3 egg whites

TO DECORATE
25 g/1 oz granulated sugar
2 tablespoons natural yogurt
50 g/2 oz low-fat soft cheese

Place the breakfast cereal in a blender or processor and blend until fine. Melt the margarine then stir in the cereal. Press the mixture into a greased 20 cm/8 inch loose-bottomed cake tin and refrigerate until firm.

Place the cheese in a bowl and mix in the honey, vanilla essence, yogurt, lemon rind and juice until smooth.

Sprinkle the gelatine over the water in a small bowl. Leave to soak for 3 minutes. Stand in a pan of simmering water and heat gently until dissolved.

Whisk the egg whites until stiff. Quickly stir the dissolved gelatine into the cheese mixture, then fold in the egg whites. Spoon over the biscuit base. Chill for about 3 hours.

Slowly dissolve the granulated sugar in a saucepan until it turns a deep caramel colour. Drizzle into irregular shapes on an oiled baking sheet. Leave to cool.

Remove the cheesecake from the tin and place on a serving dish. Beat together the soft cheese and yogurt. Spoon or pipe onto the cheesecake. Decorate with the caramel.

| ◑ medium fibre | 255 calories |
| ● low saturated fat | P:S ratio 1.5:1 |

PRUNE MOUSSE

SERVES 6

250 g/8 oz dried pitted prunes
300 ml/½ pint natural yogurt
grated rind and juice of 1 orange
1 tablespoon powdered gelatine
2 egg whites
2 tablespoons caster sugar

TO DECORATE

250 g/8 oz low-fat soft cheese
1 tablespoon clear honey
2 tablespoons chopped walnuts

Tie a band of double greaseproof paper round a 15 cm/6 inch soufflé dish to stand 5 cm/2 inches above the rim; oil the inside of the paper.

Cover the prunes with water in a small pan, bring to the boil, cover and simmer gently for 20 minutes until soft. Sieve or work in a blender with a little of the cooking liquid until smooth. Leave to cool then stir in the yogurt.

Place all but 1 tablespoon of orange juice in a small bowl and sprinkle the gelatine over the top then leave to soak for 3 minutes. Stand in a pan of simmering water and heat gently until dissolved. Quickly stir into the prune mixture.

Whisk the egg whites until stiff then whisk in the caster sugar. Carefully fold into the semi-set prune mixture.

Turn into the prepared soufflé dish and leave to set in the refrigerator.

Mix the soft cheese with the grated orange rind, remaining juice and honey. Beat until smooth, then place in a piping bag fitted with a fluted nozzle. Remove the paper from the soufflé and press the nuts round the sides. Decorate with the orange cheese.

● high fibre		195 calories
● low saturated fat		P:S ratio 1:1

PEARS in PORT

SERVES 4

1 orange
100 ml/4 fl oz port wine
250 ml/8 fl oz red grape juice
4 firm dessert pears
2 teaspoons arrowroot

Pare away the rind of the orange and cut into thin needleshreds. Squeeze the juice from the orange.

Place the port in a small saucepan with the grape juice, orange needleshreds and juice. Cover and bring to the boil.

Peel the pears, leaving on the stalks, and place in the saucepan. Baste them with the juice, cover the pan and simmer gently for 20 minutes, until the pears are tender. Cool in the liquid.

Arrange the pears on a serving dish. Mix the arrowroot with a little of the cooking liquid, then pour back into the rest of the liquid and bring to the boil, stirring. Simmer until thickened and clear. Leave to cool. Spoon over the pears and chill before serving.

This is the perfect ending to a rich meal. Chill the cooled pears for at least 2 hours to allow the flavours time to develop. Baste occasionally with the liquid to ensure a good even colour.

Desserts for special occasions: Iced lime soufflé and a handsomely decorated Vanilla cheesecake.

◐ medium fibre		120 calories
● low saturated fat		P:S ratio —

GOOSEBERRY and ELDERFLOWER SHERBET

SERVES 6

500 g/1 lb gooseberries
3 heads of elderflower or
1 tablespoon dried elderflowers
300 ml/½ pint water
4 to 6 tablespoons clear honey
1 egg white

Place the gooseberries in a pan with the elderflowers and water. Cover and simmer gently for 10 to 15 minutes until tender. Purée in a blender or processor. Add the honey to taste, then sieve and leave to cool, completely.

Turn into a rigid freezer-proof container, cover, seal and freeze for about 3 hours until half frozen.

Whisk the egg white until stiff then fold into the gooseberry mixture. Cover and re-freeze until firm. Transfer to the refrigerator for 20 minutes before scooping into chilled glasses. Decorate with elderflower or gooseberry leaves.

If both fresh and dried elderflowers are unobtainable add a few drops of rosewater to the gooseberry mixture.

◐ medium fibre	65 calories
● low saturated fat	P: S ratio —

Strawberry snowball, a luscious concoction of marinated straw-berries and a fluffy cheese 'cream'.

BROWN BREAD ICE CREAM

SERVES 6 TO 8

150 g/5 oz wholemeal
breadcrumbs, toasted
150 g/5 oz soft brown sugar
3 egg whites
300 ml/½ pint natural or
apricot yogurt

Mix together the breadcrumbs, and 50 g/2 oz of the sugar. Whisk the egg whites until stiff then gradually whisk in the remaining sugar. Fold in the yogurt and breadcrumb mixture. Turn into a rigid, freezer-proof container. Cover and freeze until firm.

Transfer to the refrigerator to soften 30 minutes before serving.

◐ medium fibre	210 calories
● low saturated fat	P: S ratio 0.7 : 1

STRAWBERRY SNOWBALL

SERVES 4

250 g/8 oz strawberries
2 tablespoons Cointreau
1 egg white
1 tablespoon caster sugar
150 ml/¼ pint smetana or
50 g/2 oz low-fat soft cheese
mixed with 50 ml/2 fl oz
natural yogurt

Reserve four strawberries for decoration. Place the remaining strawberries in a bowl, add the Cointreau and leave to marinate for 1 hour, turning them occasionally.

Whisk the egg white until stiff then whisk in the caster sugar. Fold in the smetana or cheese mixture with a few strawberries.

Layer the remaining strawberries, Cointreau and cheese mixture into four glasses. Decorate with the reserved strawberries.

◐ medium fibre	65 calories
● low saturated fat	P: S ratio —

Crunch-nut ice cream, serve by itself or with chopped fresh fruit.

CRUNCH-NUT ICE CREAM

SERVES 6 TO 8

150 g/5 oz crunchy toasted
breakfast cereal
3 egg whites
50 g/2 oz soft brown sugar
300 ml/½ pint natural yogurt

Place the cereal in a polythene bag and crush roughly with a rolling pin.

Whisk the egg whites until stiff then gradually whisk in the sugar. Mix the yogurt with a fork until smooth then fold into the egg whites with all but 1 tablespoon of the cereal. Turn into a rigid freezer-proof container, cover, seal and freeze until firm. About 3 to 4 hours.

Transfer to the refrigerator 30 minutes before serving, to soften. Scoop into chilled glasses and sprinkle the remaining cereal on top.

◐ medium fibre	155 calories	
● low saturated fat	P:S ratio 0.5:1	

WHOLEMEAL APPLE and BLACKBERRY PIE

SERVES 6

PASTRY
75 g/3 oz plain wholemeal flour
75 g/3 oz plain white flour
1 teaspoon baking powder
2 tablespoons oat bran
75 g/3 oz White Flora
2 to 3 tablespoons iced water

FILLING
500 g/1 lb dessert apples,
peeled, cored and sliced
250 g/8 oz blackberries
3 tablespoons clear honey

Place the flours, baking powder and oat bran in a bowl. Rub in the white fat until the mixture resembles breadcrumbs. Gradually add the water and mix to a firm dough. Chill for 15 minutes.

Mix the apples and blackberries together then place in a 900 ml/1½ pint pie dish and drizzle over the honey or sugar.

Turn the dough onto a floured surface and knead lightly. Roll out thinly to a round about 5 cm/2 inches larger than the pie dish. Cut off a narrow strip all round and use to cover the dampened rim of the pie dish, then brush with water.

Lift the pastry onto a rolling pin and place over the fruit, sealing the edges well. Trim and flute the edges and make a hole in the centre. Brush with water and bake in a preheated oven (200°C/400°F, Gas Mark 6) for 30 to 40 minutes. Serve hot or cold.

Sprinkle the pie with 1 teaspoon of sesame seeds before baking for an extra crispy topping.

● high fibre	265 calories	
● low saturated fat	P:S ratio 4:1	

ALMOND PLUM CRUMBLE

SERVES 6

500 g / 1 lb firm plums, halved
and stoned
300 ml / ½ pint pure
unsweetened orange juice
pinch grated nutmeg
75 g / 3 oz plain wholemeal flour
75 g / 3 oz plain white flour
50 g / 2 oz Flora margarine
50 g / 2 oz soft brown sugar
50 g / 2 oz flaked almonds

Place the plums in a saucepan with the orange juice and nutmeg. Bring to the boil and simmer for 2 minutes. Spoon the fruit mixture into an ovenproof pie dish.

Place the flours in a bowl and rub in the margarine until it resembles breadcrumbs. Stir in the sugar and almonds. Sprinkle over the fruit to cover completely.

Bake in a preheated oven (200°C/400°F, Gas Mark 6) for 25 to 30 minutes or until golden brown. Serve with Orange Custard (see page 67).

● high fibre	270 calories
● low saturated fat	P:S ratio 3:1

HAZELNUT SPONGE PUDDING

SERVES 4

3 large oranges
125 g / 4 oz hazelnuts
75 g / 3 oz soft brown sugar
2 teaspoons mixed spice
50 g / 2 oz Flora margarine
1 egg
25 g / 1 oz self-raising
wholemeal flour
50 g / 2 oz self-raising white flour
1 teaspoon icing sugar,
to decorate

Grate the orange rinds and reserve. Remove all skin and pith from the oranges using a serrated knife. Cut between the membranes to release the segments and reserve.

Brown the hazelnuts under a hot grill. Place in a tea towel and rub off the skins. Roughly chop the nuts. Mix half the nuts with 25 g/1 oz sugar and the mixed spice.

Cream together the margarine and remaining sugar until very pale and fluffy. Gradually beat in the egg. Fold in the flours, remaining nuts and half the orange rind.

Reserve eight orange segments for garnish. Place the remainder in a shallow 600 ml/ 1 pint baking dish with the nut, sugar and mixed spice mixture. Spoon over the creamed mixture and scatter over the reserved orange segments and remaining rind.

Bake in a preheated oven (190°C/375°F, Gas Mark 5) for 35 minutes or until well risen and golden. Dust with icing sugar before serving with Nutmeg Custard (see opposite).

● high fibre	400 calories
● low saturated fat	P:S ratio 3:1

GINGERED APRICOT COMPOTE

SERVES 4

125 g/4 oz dried apricots
1 kg/2 lb rhubarb, trimmed or
1 kg/2 lb greengages, halved
and stoned
25 g/1 oz preserved stem
ginger, drained and thinly sliced
1 teaspoon ground ginger
50 g/2 oz soft brown sugar

Cover the apricots with cold water and leave to soak overnight.

Cut the rhubarb into 2.5 cm/1 inch lengths if using. Place the rhubarb or greengages with both gingers in a medium-sized, oven-proof dish. Stir in the soaked apricots with 150 ml/¼ pint of the soaking liquid and the sugar. Cover tightly with foil.

Bake in a preheated oven (180°C/350°F, Gas Mark 4) for about 30 minutes.

Serve hot with a light custard (see page 76) or cool and serve with natural yogurt.

- ● high fibre
- ● low saturated fat

120 calories
P:S ratio —

SPICED BANANA PUDDING

SERVES 4

250 g/8 oz unsliced wholemeal
bread
150 g/5 oz dried bananas,
finely chopped
50 g/2 oz sultanas
450 ml/¾ pint skimmed milk
3 eggs
2 teaspoons demerara sugar
¼ teaspoon ground cinnamon
grated rind of 1 lemon
25 g/1 oz Flora margarine

Cut the bread into 2.5 cm/1 inch cubes. Mix with the bananas and sultanas.

Whisk together the milk, eggs, sugar, cinnamon and lemon rind. Pour over the bread and fruit. Stir gently.

Spoon into a shallow ovenproof dish. Dot the margarine on top. Bake in a preheated oven (170°C/325°F, Gas Mark 3) for about 1 hour. Cover with foil after 40 minutes.

- ● high fibre
- ● low saturated fat

420 calories
P:S ratio 2:1

Spiced banana pudding; Hazelnut sponge pudding with Nutmeg custard.

NUTMEG CUSTARD

SERVES 6

2 tablespoons cornflour
600 ml/1 pint skimmed milk
1 tablespoon soft brown sugar
½ teaspoon grated nutmeg

Mix the cornflour to a smooth paste with a little of the milk. Heat the remainder to boiling point. Stir in the cornflour, sugar and nutmeg. Simmer, until thickened.

- ○ low fibre
- ● low saturated fat

65 calories
P:S ratio —

CINNAMON BANANA TEA BREAD

SERVES 12

175 g/6 oz dried, pitted prunes
175 ml/6 fl oz cold tea
125 g/4 oz plain wholemeal
flour
175 g/6 oz plain white flour
1 tablespoon baking powder
2 teaspoons ground cinnamon
50 g/2 oz wholemeal
breadcrumbs, toasted
75 g/3 oz soft brown sugar
2 large bananas
120 ml/4 fl oz Flora Oil
2 eggs

Place the prunes in a bowl with the cold tea, and leave to soak for 1 hour.

Lightly oil a deep 20 cm/8 inch square cake tin and line with non-stick baking parchment. Mix together in a bowl the flour, baking powder, cinnamon and all but 1 tablespoon each of the breadcrumbs and the sugar.

Drain the prunes (reserving the soaking liquid), and roughly chop. Stir into the dry ingredients with 250 g/8 oz mashed banana.

Whisk together the reserved soaking liquid, oil and eggs. Beat into the mixture until thoroughly combined. Turn into the prepared tin. Thinly slice the remaining banana into the reserved breadcrumbs and sugar. Sprinkle over the cake mixture. Bake in a preheated oven (180°C/350°F, Gas Mark 4) for about 1 to 1¼ hours, or until the cake springs back when lightly pressed. Cool on a wire rack.

Dried prunes soaked in cold tea give this teabread a delectable moist quality and rich flavour, highlighted with a touch of spice. It will keep well for 2 to 3 days in an airtight container.

| ● high fibre | 255 calories |
| ● low saturated fat | P:S ratio 3:1 |

CARROT FRUIT CAKE

SERVES 8

125 g/4 oz soft brown sugar
6 tablespoons clear honey
175 g/6 oz carrots, finely grated
125 g/4 oz seedless raisins
50 g/2 oz stoned dates,
chopped
½ teaspoon ground mace
125 g/4 oz Flora margarine
150 ml/¼ pint water
1 egg, beaten
125 g/4 oz plain white flour
125 g/4 oz plain wholemeal
flour
2 teaspoons baking powder

TOPPING
200 g/7 oz natural quark or low-
fat soft cheese
2 tablespoons clear honey
1 teaspoon lemon juice
1 tablespoon chopped walnuts

Mix together the sugar, honey, carrots, raisins, dates, mace, margarine and water in a saucepan. Bring to the boil. Simmer gently for 5 minutes. Turn into a mixing bowl and leave until cold.

Beat in the egg. Mix together the flours and baking powder and fold into the fruit mixture until thoroughly combined.

Lightly oil a 23 cm/9 inch cake tin. Line with non-stick baking parchment. Turn the mixture into the prepared tin and level the surface. Bake in a preheated oven (180°C/350°F, Gas Mark 4) for 55 to 60 minutes, or until firm. Cool on a wire rack.

Beat together all the topping ingredients except the walnuts. Spread evenly over the surface of the cooled cake. Sprinkle over the walnuts.

The natural sweetness of carrots combines well with raisins and dates to produce a taste and texture that will make this cake a firm favourite for special occasions.

Easy to make Carrot fruit cake with honey topping, a special treat for special occasions.

| ● high fibre | 440 calories |
| ● low saturated fat | P:S ratio 3:1 |

Malted oat squares; Lemon and nutmeg digestives.

LEMON and NUTMEG DIGESTIVES

MAKES 24

*175 g/6 oz self-raising
wholemeal flour
50 g/2 oz fine oatmeal
a little salt
grated rind of 1 lemon
1/4 teaspoon grated nutmeg
75 g/3 oz Flora margarine
25 g/1 oz soft brown sugar
2 to 4 tablespoons
skimmed milk
grated nutmeg, to decorate*

Mix together the flour, oatmeal, salt, lemon rind and nutmeg. Rub in the margarine until the mixture resembles breadcrumbs. Stir in the sugar. Add the milk and mix to a firm dough.

Turn onto a floured surface and roll out thinly. Stamp out 24 rounds with a 6 cm/2½ inch plain cutter. Place on a non-stick baking sheet and prick with a fork. Brush with water and sprinkle with grated nutmeg.

Bake in a preheated oven (190°C/375°F, Gas Mark 5) for 15 to 20 minutes. Cool on a wire rack.

These biscuits have a light, crisp texture with a delicate flavour of citrus and spice. Ideal to serve with coffee or as an extra with fresh fruit salads. For a party they look pretty if differently shaped cutters are used. For a subtle variation try orange rind and allspice or lime with ground ginger.

| ◑ medium fibre | 60 calories |
| ● low saturated fat | P:S ratio 3:1 |

MALTED OAT SQUARES

MAKES 16

*120 ml/4 fl oz Flora Oil
3 tablespoons malt extract
50 g/2 oz soft brown sugar
250 g/8 oz rolled oats
2 tablespoons sesame seeds,
toasted*

Place the oil, malt extract and sugar in a saucepan and heat gently stirring all the time. Add the rolled oats and toasted sesame seeds and mix quickly and thoroughly until well blended.

Press the mixture evenly into a lightly oiled 20 cm/8 inch square shallow cake tin. Bake in a preheated oven (180°C/350°F, Gas Mark 4) for 20 to 30 minutes or until golden brown and firm to the touch.

Cool in the tin for 2 minutes then cut into squares. Cool completely before carefully removing from the tin.

| ◑ medium fibre | 165 calories |
| ● low saturated fat | P:S ratio 5:1 |

CRACKED WHEAT PLAIT

MAKES 1 LOAF

125 g/4 oz cracked wheat
15 g/½ oz fresh yeast or
1 tablespoon dried yeast
300 ml/½ pint tepid water
250 g/8 oz plain wholemeal
flour
200 g/7 oz strong, plain
white flour
a little salt
25 g/1 oz White Flora

Cover the cracked wheat with cold water and leave to soak for 1 hour. Drain well.

Crumble the fresh yeast into the water and leave for 20 minutes until frothy. (If using dried yeast follow the manufacturer's instructions for reconstituting.) Mix together the flours, salt and wheat. Rub in the white fat. Stir in the yeast liquid and mix to a soft dough. Knead on a floured surface until smooth and elastic. Place in an oiled polythene bag and leave in a warm place for about 1 hour until doubled in size.

Divide the dough into three equal pieces and roll each to a 30 cm/12 inch length. Plait together. Place on a floured baking sheet. Cover with a damp tea towel and leave to rise in a warm place for about 25 minutes. Brush with egg or milk. Bake in a preheated oven (220°C/425°F, Gas Mark 7) for 25 to 30 minutes, or until the bottom sounds hollow when tapped. Cool on a wire rack.

| ● high fibre | 212 calories |
| ● low saturated fat | P:S ratio 4:1 |

WHOLEMEAL COTTAGE LOAF

MAKES 1 LOAF

15 g/½ oz fresh yeast or
1 tablespoon dried yeast
450 ml/¾ pint lukewarm water
500 g/1 lb plain wholemeal
flour
250 g/8 oz plain white flour
a little salt
25 g/1 oz Flora margarine
1 tablespoon malt extract
skimmed milk, to glaze

Prepare the yeast as for Cracked Wheat Plait (see above). Mix together the flours and salt. Rub in the margarine. Stir in the yeast liquid and the malt extract. Mix to a soft dough.

Knead on a floured surface until smooth and elastic. Place in an oiled polythene bag and leave to rise in a warm place for about 1 hour or until doubled in size.

Knead again for 1 to 2 minutes then cut off a third of the dough. Shape the larger portion into an even round and place on a floured baking sheet. Shape the remaining dough into a small, even round. Moisten the top of the larger round and place the smaller one on top. Push the floured handle of a wooden spoon through the centre to secure them together. Cover with a damp tea towel and leave to rise in a warm place for about 25 minutes.

Finish and bake as for Cracked Wheat Plait (see above).

| ● high fibre | 277 calories |
| ● low saturated fat | P:S ratio 4:1 |

RYE and ONION BREAD

MAKES 8

15 g/½ oz fresh yeast or
1 tablespoon dried yeast
300 ml/½ pint tepid water
175 g/6 oz plain wholemeal
flour
250 g/8 oz rye flour
a little salt
3 teaspoons caraway seeds
1 tablespoon molasses
2 tablespoons Flora Oil
250 g/8 oz onion, chopped

Prepare the yeast as for Cracked Wheat Plait (see above). Mix together the flours, salt and 2 teaspoons of the caraway seeds. Stir in the yeast liquid, molasses and 1 tablespoon of the oil. Mix to a soft dough.

Knead on a floured surface until smooth and elastic. Place in an oiled polythene bag and leave in a warm place for about 2 hours or until doubled in size.

Knead again for 1 to 2 minutes. Shape into eight even rounds. Place together in a large round (see photograph) on a baking sheet. Cover with a damp tea towel and leave to rise in a warm place for 20 to 25 minutes.

Meanwhile sauté the onions in the remaining oil until soft. Brush the bread with egg and sprinkle with the remaining caraway seeds, and onion. Brush again with egg.

Bake in a preheated oven (220°C/425°F, Gas Mark 7) for 15 minutes. Lower the heat to (190°C/375°F, Gas Mark 5) and bake for a further 10 to 15 minutes. Cover with foil if necessary. Cool on a wire rack.

| ● high fibre | 240 calories |
| ● low saturated fat | P:S ratio 5:1 |

Quick savoury scone, a fast mix for impromptu meals; Rye and onion bread.

QUICK SAVOURY SCONE

SERVES 8

250 g/8 oz plain white flour
1 teaspoon cream of tartar
½ teaspoon bicarbonate of soda
a little salt
1 teaspoon English
mustard powder
good pinch of cayenne pepper
50 g/2 oz Flora margarine
125 g/4 oz Edam cheese, grated
1 teaspoon dried sage
about 150 ml/¼ pint skimmed
milk

Place the flour in a mixing bowl then sift in the raising agents, salt, mustard and pepper. Rub in the margarine until it resembles breadcrumbs. Reserve 25 g/1 oz of the cheese then stir in the rest with the sage. Add enough milk to mix to a soft dough.

Turn the dough onto a floured surface, knead lightly.

Divide the dough into three equal pieces and roll each to a 20 cm/8 inch length. Plait together. Place on a floured baking sheet. Brush the top with water and sprinkle over the remaining cheese.

Bake in a preheated oven (200°C/400°F,

Gas Mark 6) for 15 to 20 minutes until golden brown and firm to the touch. Cool on a wire rack.

To make a simple scone round, shape the dough into an 18 cm/7 inch round and place on a floured baking sheet. Score the round into 8 sections using a sharp knife. Finish and bake as above.

◐ medium fibre	200 calories	
◑ med. saturated fat	P:S ratio 1:1	

47

Left: Spicy drumsticks (recipe page 51)

These mildly spiced chicken portions are a tasty idea for picnics or barbecues. Ideal too as party food garnished with Toadstool eggs.

Below, left to right: Summer salad; Fruity coleslaw; Carrot and cress salad (recipes page 53).

Good eating habits are best learnt at an early age so they become second nature to children as they grow up. To encourage them to eat well it is important to present their food as temptingly as possible. Small attractively served portions will have more appeal than large off-putting platefuls. They can always come back for seconds. It's also a good idea to involve the children, as much as possible, both in choosing and cooking their food. The recipes in this chapter are both fun and nutritious and many have

the added bonus of being simple enough for children to prepare themselves. Try and set aside one day a week – or if that's impossible – one meal a week – when everyone makes a contribution. Even a toddler can help lay the table or add the finishing touches to a pudding.

Between meals

Many of the snacks children enjoy are high in the things we're encouraged to eat less of i.e. saturated fat, salt and sugar. A bag of potato crisps occasionally won't do much harm but shouldn't be made a daily habit. Encourage children from the earliest possible age to eat more of the right kinds of foods. When faced with a kitchen full of ravenous children newly arrived home from school offer a piece of fresh or dried fruit, cubes of Edam cheese, or sticks of raw vegetables to munch on instead of sweets or crisps.

Packed for health

School lunches are not always very popular with children and have a tendency towards 'Chips with everything'. A good alternative is a packed lunch. It's easy to keep the basic ingredients in stock, make small alterations daily and the lunch pack is ready in minutes. Above all try to combine your desire for good nutrition with their desire for conformity with their friends. It must be just as appealing as any other meal but try not to be too unusual.

Portion control

Try and keep everything to a manageable size, simple and quick to eat. Young children, especially, prefer individual packages. Things like packets of raisins, small cartons of pure unsweetened fruit juice, pots of crunchy colourful salads and individual savoury tarts will all be popular. Vegetable crudités with small containers of savoury dip are also fun to eat. (See page 51 for some Dip Stick ideas that are sure to become firm favourites.)

Sandwiches and rolls are always welcome and easy to pack and transport. Although some children do not like wholemeal bread, it is more nourishing than white. It's a good idea to meet them halfway and make finger sandwiches or triple-deckers with alternate slices of white and brown bread. Keep a stock of interesting sandwich fillings in the refrigerator and ring the changes from day to day.

Alternatively, make up a batch of sandwiches with simple fillings such as grated cheese, tuna fish, lean ham or chicken and freeze in useful portions. These can be defrosted overnight in the refrigerator ready to wrap and pack in the morning.

Shredded lettuce can be tossed together with several crisp ingredients, mixing sweet and savoury together with light dressings to make interesting salads. Try pots of:

- cubed cooked turkey, chopped pineapple and pasta shells with a little vinaigrette dressing or herb mayonnaise (see page 77)
- cubes of Edam or Feta cheese, cucumber and melon
- shredded lean ham with chopped celery, apple, peanuts and raisins and a little natural yogurt to moisten
- mixed cooked beans, segments of orange, thinly sliced onion and vinaigrette dressing (see page 77).

It is inevitable that children will look for something sweet in their lunch packs. A piece of fresh fruit is the healthiest and most convenient 'sweet' to pack. Small cakes and biscuits may be included occasionally and will be especially welcomed if they are home-made. (Try the recipes on pages 54 and 55.) They are often lower in sugar and saturated fat and can be cheaper than bought ones.

Try these recipes when cooking for kids. They're sure to meet with approval while helping your children towards a healthier pattern of eating.

SURPRISE BURGERS

MAKES 8

25 g/1 oz Flora margarine
1 onion, finely chopped
1 leek, finely chopped
2 sticks celery, finely chopped
2 carrots, finely chopped
1 clove garlic, crushed
500 g/1 lb mashed potato
2 tablespoons chopped
fresh parsley
1 tablespoon tomato paste
1 teaspoon dried mixed herbs
freshly ground black pepper
wholemeal flour, for coating
1 to 2 tablespoons Flora Oil,
for cooking

Melt the margarine in a saucepan and stir in the chopped vegetables and garlic. Cook, stirring, over a low heat for about 8 to 10 minutes until softened but not brown. Cool slightly.

Add the sautéed vegetables to the potato with the parsley, tomato paste, mixed herbs and pepper. Mix well until thoroughly combined.

Divide the mixture into eight. Shape into small rounds and flatten slightly into 'burgers'. Coat lightly in wholemeal flour. Place on a baking sheet, cover and chill for 30 minutes.

Heat the oil in a shallow sauté pan. Cook the vegburgers on both sides for 10 minutes or until golden and hot through. Pat dry on absorbent kitchen paper before serving.

Make a simple barbecue sauce to serve with the burgers for a quick teatime treat:

Place 125 g/4 oz onion and a 226 g/8 oz can tomatoes in a blender or processor with 2 tablespoons each tomato paste, Flora Oil, white wine vinegar, soft brown sugar, English mustard powder and Worcestershire sauce. Blend until smooth, bring to the boil and simmer for 10 minutes while the 'burgers' are cooking.

To complete the meal serve an equally simple salad such as Carrot and Cress Salad (see page 53).

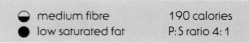

◐ medium fibre	190 calories	
● low saturated fat	P:S ratio 4:1	

DID YOU KNOW...?

It takes 500 g/1 lb of potatoes to make 125 g/4 oz of crisps. On the way the potatoes lose valuable fibre and vitamins and gain salt and saturated fat.

The shape of potato chips can make a difference to their fat content. Some potato chips will have more fat than others. Crinkle-cut chips, with their increased surface area, absorb more fat when cooked than thick, straight-cut chips.

Quiche is often considered a 'healthy' food, but a 125 g/4 oz slice can contain almost as much fat as 125 g/4 oz Danish Blue cheese.

Our usage of vitamin C varies with lifestyle. For example, both stress and smoking use up this vitamin. Our bodies barely store vitamin C and so daily supplies, in the form of fruit and vegetables, are sensible.

Spinach is not exceptionally high in iron whatever Popeye claims. Scientists in the 19th century misplaced the decimal point crediting spinach with 10 times its real iron content.

FASTA PIZZA

MAKES 10

SCONE BASE
125 g/4 oz self-raising
wholemeal flour
125 g/4 oz self-raising
white flour
1 teaspoon dried mixed herbs
50 g/2 oz Flora margarine
120 ml/4 fl oz skimmed milk

TOPPING
25 g/1 oz Flora margarine
1 onion, chopped
397 g/14 oz can tomatoes,
drained and chopped
50 g/2 oz lean ham, diced
½ teaspoon dried marjoram
freshly ground black pepper
125 g/4 oz Edam cheese, grated
5 black olives, stoned
and chopped
10 anchovies, drained and
halved (optional)

Place the scone ingredients in a bowl and blend together with a fork to form a soft dough.

Turn onto a lightly floured surface, knead very gently and press out to 1 cm/½ inch thick. Stamp out five 7.5 cm/3 inch rounds with a plain cutter and place on a lightly floured baking sheet. Bake in a preheated oven (220°C/425°F, Gas Mark 7) for 10 to 12 minutes until golden. Cool on a wire rack.

Make the topping. Melt the margarine in a saucepan and fry the onion until softened. Add the tomatoes, ham, marjoram and pepper and cook for 3 minutes or until most of the excess liquid has evaporated.

Cut the scones in half and place on a grill pan. Place a spoonful of the tomato mixture on each half. Sprinkle with the cheese and a little chopped olive. If using anchovies arrange in a lattice pattern.

Place under a preheated grill for 12 to 15 minutes until golden and bubbling.

◐ medium fibre	225 calories	
◐ med. saturated fat	P:S ratio 1:1	

DIP STICKS

SERVES 4

125 g/4 oz fromage frais or low-
fat soft cheese
2 tablespoons smooth
peanut butter
1 clove garlic, crushed
freshly ground black pepper

DIPPERS
cauliflower
carrot
celery
red pepper

Place the cheese in a bowl and mix in the peanut butter, garlic and pepper. Pack into small, individual plastic containers. Choose a selection of vegetables as liked from those listed for dipping. Cut the cauliflower into florets and the other vegetables into sticks measuring about 1 × 7.5 cm/½ × 3 inches and wrap in cling film.

Optional Extras: try adding one of the following to the cheese mixture.

2 tablespoons mango chutney

2 tablespoons mild burger mustard with finely chopped onion

3 tablespoons finely chopped lean ham or chicken with chopped parsley

2 rashers lean bacon, trimmed, grilled until crisp, and crumbled

2 tablespoons chopped fresh chives and 1 tablespoon chopped cucumber

1 teaspoon mild curry paste and 1 tablespoon mayonnaise

| ● high fibre | 150 calories |
| ◐ med. saturated fat | P:S ratio 1:1 |

SPICY DRUMSTICKS

MAKES 8

8 chicken drumsticks
3 tablespoons natural yogurt
1 teaspoon each coriander,
paprika, and ginger
½ teaspoon cumin
1 clove garlic, crushed
2 tablespoons Flora Oil

Remove the skin from the drumsticks. With a sharp knife make 2 deep cuts in the flesh of each one.

Mix the yogurt with the spices, garlic and oil and use to coat the drumsticks. Place in a single layer on a shallow heatproof dish. Cover and leave to marinate in the refrigerator for 2 hours.

Grill the drumsticks, basting with the marinade, for about 8 to 10 minutes on each side or until cooked. Test with a skewer. The juices should run clear. Serve hot or cold.

Serve Toadstool Eggs with the drumsticks. Halve and de-seed 4 tomatoes. Cut a slice from the base of 8 hard-boiled eggs. Stand on a flat plate. Top each egg with a tomato half. Fill a greaseproof paper piping bag with polyunsaturated margarine, dot the tomatoes as shown on page 48.

| ○ low fibre | 80 calories |
| ◐ med. saturated fat | P:S ratio 2:1 |

SUPPER TOASTIES

MAKES 12

4 large slices wholemeal bread
25 g/1 oz Flora margarine
4 thin slices lean ham
125 g/4 oz Edam cheese,
thinly sliced

Toast the bread then spread with the margarine. Lay a slice of ham on each piece of toast then cover with a slice of cheese.

Place under a preheated hot grill and cook until the cheese is golden and bubbling. Remove from the grill, cut each piece into 3 fingers and serve immediately garnished with watercress or parsley sprigs.

Alternatively, omit the ham and put either a little cooked chicken, sliced tomatoes, thinly sliced onion or a ring of fresh pineapple on the toast before covering with cheese.

Wholemeal muffins, scones and crumpets can also be topped and toasted in this way. Split them in half before using.

| ◐ medium fibre | 95 calories |
| ◐ med. saturated fat | P:S ratio 0.7:1 |

TUG-BOAT EGGS

MAKES 8

4 hard-boiled eggs
90 g/3½ oz can tuna fish in brine, drained
1 tablespoon natural yogurt
2 tablespoons mayonnaise
freshly ground black pepper
2.5 cm/1 inch piece of cucumber (or celery)
1 carrot
8 bayleaves

Halve the eggs lengthwise, scoop out the yolks and sieve into a mixing bowl. Add the tuna fish to the yolks with the yogurt, mayonnaise and pepper to taste. Mix with a fork until very smooth.

Cut a slice from the bottom of each egg half so that it will stand evenly. Put a spoonful of tuna mixture on each egg and shape into a mould with a palette knife.

Cut the cucumber into eight 2.5 cm/1 inch sticks and press one stick upright into each egg. Cut the carrot into 2.5 cm/1 inch sticks and place in front of the cucumber to resemble funnels. Press in the bayleaves to resemble sails. Arrange on a bed of finely shredded lettuce and beansprouts, to serve.

| ○ low fibre | 80 calories |
| ◐ med. saturated fat | P:S ratio 0.8 : 1 |

SWEETCORN TARTLETS

MAKES 14

PASTRY
50 g/2 oz White Flora
2 tablespoons water
125 g/4 oz plain or wholemeal flour

FILLING
1 tablespoon Flora Oil
1 onion, finely chopped
1 stick celery, finely chopped
1 egg
75 ml/3 fl oz skimmed milk
75 g/3 oz sweetcorn kernels
75 g/3 oz Brie or Edam cheese, rinded and cubed
freshly ground black pepper

Place the white fat, water and 1 tablespoon of the flour in a bowl and mix together with a fork. Stir in the remaining flour and mix to a firm dough. Turn onto a lightly floured surface and knead gently until smooth. Chill for 20 minutes.

Heat the oil in a pan and fry the onion and celery for about 3 to 4 minutes until softened but not coloured. Leave to cool slightly. Mix the egg and milk together in a bowl then stir in the sweetcorn, onion, celery, cheese and pepper.

Roll the pastry out very thinly. Stamp out fourteen 7.5 cm/3 inch rounds and use to line small tartlet tins. Spoon the filling into the pastry cases and bake in a preheated oven (200°C/400°F, Gas Mark 6) for 20 to 25 minutes, or until golden and just set.

| ◐ medium fibre | 95 calories |
| ● low saturated fat | P:S ratio 3 : 1 |

Food for the very young: Tug-boat eggs and Sweetcorn tartlets.

CARROT and CRESS SALAD

SERVES 4

500 g/1 lb carrots, scrubbed
1 box mustard and cress
4 tablespoons French Dressing
(see page 77)

Grate the carrots finely then place them in a bowl with the mustard and cress. Pour over the dressing, toss thoroughly and leave to stand for 30 minutes before serving.

| ● high fibre | 95 calories |
| ● low saturated fat | P:S ratio 4:1 |

SUMMER SALAD

SERVES 4

1 stick of celery, diced
¼ cucumber, diced
2 tomatoes, chopped
75 g/3 oz Edam or Feta
cheese, cubed
a little shredded lettuce
2 tablespoons French Dressing
(see page 77)

Place all the ingredients in a bowl and toss well. Serve garnished with chopped chives.

If packing for lunches or picnics, omit the lettuce and stir in a little shredded cabbage.

| ○ low fibre | 130 calories |
| ◐ med. saturated fat | P:S ratio 1:1 |

FRUITY COLESLAW

SERVES 4

DRESSING
3 tablespoons Flora Oil
2 teaspoons lemon juice
2 teaspoons pure unsweetened
apple juice
½ teaspoon mild mustard
a little salt
freshly ground black pepper

SALAD
1 red dessert apple, cored
1 orange
50 g/2 oz each black and green
grapes, halved and seeded
125 g/4 oz white cabbage,
finely shredded
1 bunch watercress, chopped

Whisk together the dressing ingredients. Slice the apply thinly into the dressing and toss thoroughly until coated. Remove the peel and pith from the orange, slice then cut into quarters. Add to the bowl with all the remaining ingredients, toss well and transfer to a salad bowl.

Grated carrot and chopped spring onions may be added in place of the grapes to make a more traditional coleslaw.

This colourful salad is a good choice for lunch boxes. It is refreshing and crisp and 'travels' well if carried in airtight containers.

| ◐ medium fibre | 140 calories |
| ● low saturated fat | P:S ratio 4:1 |

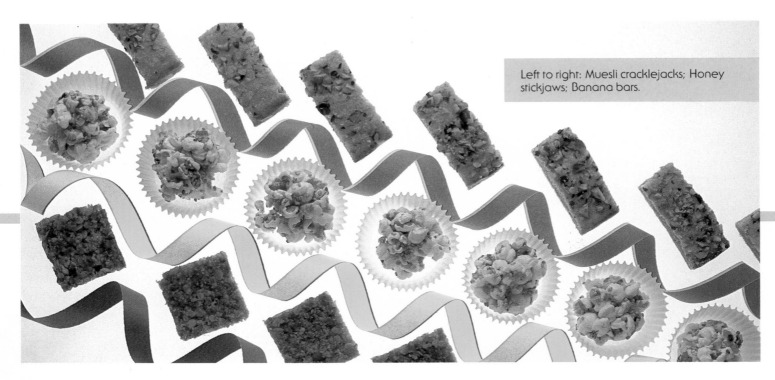

Left to right: Muesli cracklejacks; Honey stickjaws; Banana bars.

MUESLI CRACKLEJACKS

MAKES 20

50 g/2 oz Flora margarine
2 tablespoons clear honey
125 g/4 oz unsweetened muesli
25 g/1 oz medium oatmeal,
toasted

Melt the margarine with the honey in a small saucepan. Stir in the muesli and oatmeal and mix together thoroughly. Turn into a greased 18 cm/7 inch square baking tin and press down firmly and evenly with a palette knife.

Bake in a preheated oven (180°C/350°F, Gas Mark 4) for 25 to 30 minutes or until golden brown. Cool in the tin for 2 minutes then cut into squares. Cool completely before carefully removing from the tin.

These crisp, crunchy biscuits are quick and easy to make and ideal for children's parties and picnics. Keep them fresh in airtight containers layered with greaseproof paper, or make in batches and freeze.

| ○ low fibre | 55 calories |
| ● low saturated fat | P:S ratio 4:1 |

HONEY STICKJAWS

MAKES 20

2 tablespoons Flora Oil
25 g/1 oz popcorn kernels
1 tablespoon clear honey
1 tablespoon sesame
seeds, toasted

Heat the oil in a large heavy-based pan. Add the popcorn, cover and cook, shaking the pan constantly until the kernels have popped. Turn the popcorn into a bowl.

Place the honey in a pan and bring to the boil. Boil for 30 seconds then stir in the popcorn and sesame seeds until evenly coated. Form into small balls with dampened fingers. Place in small paper cases. Leave

to cool at room temperature for 20 to 30 minutes or until set.

| ○ low fibre | 25 calories |
| ● low saturated fat | P:S ratio 5:1 |

COCONUT CRISPS

MAKES 20

25 g/1 oz soft brown sugar
50 g/2 oz Flora margarine
1 egg
25 g/1 oz rolled oats
75 g/3 oz plain wholemeal flour
1 teaspoon baking powder
25 g/1 oz desiccated coconut

Sieve the sugar. Add the margarine and cream together until very light and fluffy. Gradually beat in the egg. Fold in the rolled oats, flour, and baking powder. Shape into small walnut-size balls and roll in the desiccated coconut.

Place the balls slightly apart on a non-stick baking sheet and flatten with a palette knife. Bake in a preheated oven (190°C/375°F, Gas Mark 5) for 10 to 15 minutes until pale golden. Cool on a wire rack.

Variation: omit the coconut and roll the mixture in one of the following:

25 g/1 oz coarse oatmeal, toasted

25 g/1 oz ground almonds

25 g/1 oz sesame seeds, toasted

| ◖ medium fibre | 50 calories |
| ◓ med. saturated fat | P:S ratio 1:1 |

BANANA BARS

MAKES 14

75 g/3 oz Flora margarine
50 g/2 oz soft brown sugar
50 g/2 oz plain wholemeal flour
75 g/3 oz plain white flour
1 teaspoon baking powder
pinch ground mixed spice
2 eggs
2 bananas, mashed
15 g/1/2 oz hazelnuts,
finely chopped

Place all the ingredients except the hazelnuts in a mixing bowl and beat vigorously for about 2 minutes until blended.

Turn the mixture into a lightly oiled 20 cm/8 inch square shallow tin lined with non-stick baking parchment. Spread evenly and sprinkle with the hazelnuts. Bake in a preheated oven (190°C/375°F, Gas Mark 5) for 25 to 30 minutes until the cake springs back when lightly pressed.

Leave in the tin for 2 minutes then cut into 14 bars. Cool on a wire rack.

Banana Bars are best eaten fresh but will keep in an airtight container for 1 to 2 days.

For an extra special treat, make up the Carrot Fruit Cake topping on page 44. Bake the Banana Bar mixture without the hazelnuts. Cool. Spread with topping and sprinkle with hazelnuts before cutting into bars.

| ◖ medium fibre | 120 calories |
| ● low saturated fat | P:S ratio 3:1 |

WALNUT DREAM CUPS

MAKES 12

1 small dessert apple
75 g/3 oz self-raising white flour
75 g/3 oz self-raising
wholemeal flour
1 teaspoon ground cinnamon
50 g/2 oz Flora margarine
2 tablespoons clear honey
4 tablespoons pure
unsweetened apple juice
1 egg
50 g/2 oz walnuts, chopped

Peel, core and coarsely grate the apple into a mixing bowl. Add all the remaining ingredients except 2 tablespoons of the walnuts and beat together thoroughly for about 2 minutes until smooth.

Arrange 12 paper cases on a baking sheet and three-quarters fill each one with the mixture. Sprinkle with the reserved walnuts then bake in a preheated oven (180°C/350°F, Gas Mark 4) for 15 to 20 minutes until golden. Cool on a wire rack.

This recipe can also be used as a baked topping on stewed fruit such as apples, rhubarb or pears. Lightly stew 500 g/1 lb prepared fruit with 1 to 2 tablespoons of soft brown sugar. Cool. Spoon into a small pie dish. Prepare the cake mixture as directed and spoon evenly over the fruit. Sprinkle with the reserved nuts and bake at (180°C/350°F, Gas Mark 4) for 20 to 25 minutes. Serve immediately.

| ◖ medium fibre | 120 calories |
| ● low saturated fat | P:S ratio 4:1 |

YOG LOLLIES

MAKES 4

*175 ml/6 fl oz pure
unsweetened orange juice
300 ml/½ pint low-fat fruit
yogurt, such as apricot or peach
½ teaspoon vanilla essence*

APPLE FROTH

SERVES 4

*500 g/1 lb dessert apples,
peeled and cored
3 tablespoons apple juice
2 egg whites
25 g/1 oz caster sugar*

Orange apple castles: fresh orange segments set in pure, unsweetened apple juice.

ORANGE APPLE CASTLES

MAKES 6

*4 oranges
300 ml/½ pint clear
unsweetened apple juice
1 tablespoon powdered gelatine*

Peel the oranges, cut into segments making sure you catch the juices, and arrange in six small ramekins.

Put 150 ml/¼ pint of the apple juice in a small saucepan, sprinkle over the gelatine and leave to soak for 3 minutes. Heat the gelatine gently until dissolved, add the remaining apple juice and any orange juice.

Pour over the oranges in the ramekins and leave to set in the refrigerator.

Dip the ramekins briefly in hot water then turn out onto a small plate to serve.

| ○ low fibre | 60 calories |
| ● low saturated fat | P:S ratio — |

NUT and APRICOT DELIGHT

SERVES 4

*300 ml/½ pint natural yogurt
50 g/2 oz dried apricots,
chopped
25 g/1 oz chopped hazelnuts,
browned*

Place the yogurt in a bowl with the apricots. Cover and leave overnight in the refrigerator.

Fold the nuts into the yogurt mixture and spoon into individual glasses.

This is a surprisingly simple but delicious concoction. It is important to leave the mixture overnight to allow the dried apricots time to plump up in the yogurt. No additional sugar is necessary as the dried fruit imparts its own natural sweetness.

| ◐ medium fibre | 85 calories |
| ● low saturated fat | P:S ratio 0.4:1 |

CHOCOLATE MINT FROTH

SERVES 2

25 g/1 oz chocolate mint bar,
grated or finely chopped
300 ml/½ pint skimmed milk

Whisk together all the ingredients and pour into divided ice cube trays, or into very small paper cups. Freeze until mushy then insert a small wooden stick into each. Return to the freezer and freeze until firm.

Place all but 1 teaspoon of the chocolate in a blender. Heat the milk. Pour into the blender or processor and blend until frothy. Serve sprinkled with the remaining chocolate.

| ○ low fibre | 90 calories |
| ● low saturated fat | P:S ratio — |

| ○ low fibre | 210 calories |
| ● low saturated fat | P:S ratio — |

BERRY SHAKE

SERVES 2

300 ml/½ pint cold
skimmed milk
75 g/3 oz raspberries, hulled, or
any soft fruits
1 tablespoon clear honey
3 tablespoons smetana, or low-
fat natural yogurt

Slice the apples into a pan, pour in the apple juice, cover and simmer for 10 to 15 minutes. Cool slightly then blend until smooth.
  Whisk the egg whites until stiff then whisk in the sugar. Fold into the apple mixture and spoon into individual dishes to serve. Decorate with mint sprigs. Serve immediately.

Place half the milk in a blender or processor with the raspberries and blend until smooth, then strain. Return to the blender or processor with the remaining ingredients and blend for a further 15 seconds. Pour into tall glasses and serve immediately.

| ◐ medium fibre | 75 calories |
| ● low saturated fat | P:S ratio — |

| ◐ medium fibre | 105 calories |
| ● low saturated fat | P:S ratio — |

BANANA YOGNOG

SERVES 2

150 ml/¼ pint cold
skimmed milk
150 ml/¼ pint natural yogurt
1 large banana
2 teaspoons soft brown sugar
pinch grated nutmeg

Place all the ingredients in a blender or processor and blend until smooth and frothy. Pour into glasses and serve immediately.

| ◐ medium fibre | 140 calories |
| ● low saturated fat | P:S ratio — |

TOMATO and CELERY WHIZZ

SERVES 2

2 sticks celery, chopped
2 carrots, grated
½ teaspoon soy sauce
150 ml/¼ pint cold water
1 tablespoon chopped chives
150 ml/¼ pint tomato juice

Place the vegetables, soy sauce, water and chives in a blender or processor. Blend until smooth then strain. Mix with the tomato juice, and serve chilled.

| ◐ medium fibre | 30 calories |
| ● low saturated fat | P:S ratio — |

FITNESS FACTS

Regular exercise not only makes you feel better — it also makes your body function better too. But don't panic! To keep fit, you don't have to run a marathon everyday. Exercise briskly for about 15 to 20 minutes three times a week and you will soon see the difference it makes. Any kind of exercise will do. Try getting off the bus a stop earlier, take a walk through the park, or use the stairs rather than the lift. Combine some regular exercise with healthy eating and you'll soon notice the improvement in your well-being. You will also find it's easier to stay slim. Regular exercise can be a blessing for dieters — it can actually reduce your appetite. You may find yourself getting hungry only when you need nourishment, not when you fancy an extra bite between meals.

Left: Carrot and lentil soup (recipe page 64).

Green cardamoms with their subtle aromatic flavour are a delightful addition to this simple soup. The perfect prelude to a traditional Sunday roast.

MENUS FOR ENTERTAINING

When family and friends gather together, whatever the occasion, there's a party to cater for. It could be a lazy Sunday lunch or a mid-summer celebration buffet, but whatever the event, we want to prepare something special and will probably splash out on ingredients we wouldn't buy regularly. In the past this has meant rich dishes prepared with lots of butter, cream and eggs and probably more food than anyone could manage comfortably. But such over-indulgence isn't necessary in order to impress or satisfy. What

matters most is that the food is attractive, appetizing and tastes delectable. Whether we're planning to present a variation on a familiar theme, or a new and unusual idea to tempt the palate; entertaining and healthy eating can go hand in hand. After all, today's most famous chefs are using the principles of less saturated fat, sugar and salt and more dietary fibre to produce fabulous results. The following menus are undeniably more indulgent than everyday meals but every bit as healthy.

Perfect planning

Choosing foods which both contrast and complement each other in texture, flavour and colour is an essential part of menu-planning. Whatever the menu, it should contain three or more well-balanced courses.

Aim for balance in the weight of the courses. Plan a light salad starter before a heavy main course or a light main dish

before a substantial pudding. The 'wet' and 'dry' rule is a good one to follow; that is, a 'wet' course such as a soup or a casserole should precede a 'dry' course such as roast beef or a pastry pudding.

Flavour balance is the next consideration. Don't paralyse the palate with hot, spicy sauces before serving delicately flavoured fish or chicken.

Fresh fruit and vegetables add colour and texture to any menu so provide a good selection of both. Vegetables should be lightly cooked to preserve their colour, texture and goodness. Fresh fruit will always provide a refreshing end to a meal. When time is limited a platter of prepared fruits served on a bed of crushed ice will provide a simple and colourful dessert.

Most people like to include cheese in their meal, either before or after the pudding. It's probably best just to offer one or two good cheeses such as a perfect wedge of Brie and a piece of Edam.

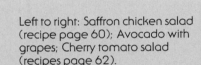

Left to right: Saffron chicken salad (recipe page 60); Avocado with grapes; Cherry tomato salad (recipes page 62).

Feeding a crowd calls for clever culinary tactics so always consider arranging a meal buffet-style when catering for larger numbers. Choose dishes which can be prepared well in advance to ensure that the occasion will be relaxed for both the guests and the hostess.

Right: Passion fruit Pavlova (recipe page 73).

For sheer indulgence, though not after a rich main course, try this delicious variation on the classic Pavlova which can be assembled well ahead of serving.

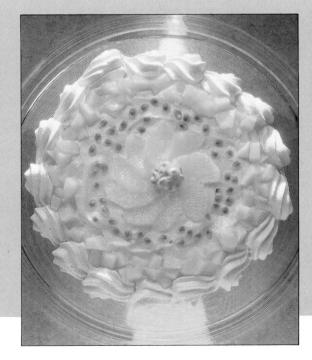

CELEBRATION BUFFET for TWELVE

SAFFRON CHICKEN SALAD – SEAFOOD VINAIGRETTE
AVOCADO WITH GRAPES – CHERRY TOMATO SALAD
HOT CHEESE BREAD
PEACHES WITH KIWI FRUIT
BAKED CHERRY CHEESECAKE

SAFFRON CHICKEN SALAD

1 egg yolk
½ teaspoon English mustard powder
½ teaspoon caster sugar
1 tablespoon white wine vinegar
Flora Oil
125 g/4 oz onion, chopped
few strands saffron
1 teaspoon ground turmeric
1 tablespoon curry powder
grated rind and 4 tablespoons juice of 1 orange
1 tablespoon tomato paste
150 ml/¼ pint white wine
2 tablespoons apricot jam
150 ml/¼ pint natural yogurt
a little salt
freshly ground black pepper
two 1½ kg/3 lb oven-ready chickens or one 2.7 kg/6 lb turkey
slices of lemon and onion and 1 bayleaf for flavouring
125 g/4 oz walnut halves
500 g/1 lb French beans, cooked

Place the egg yolk in a medium bowl. Whisk in the mustard, sugar and vinegar. Then very gradually whisk in 200 ml/⅓ pint of the oil until the mixture is very thick and smooth. Cover and refrigerate.

Sauté the onion in 1 tablespoon of oil for 3 to 4 minutes until soft and golden. Stir in the saffron, turmeric and curry powder. Cook, stirring, for 1 minute before adding the orange rind and juice, tomato paste and wine. Simmer, uncovered, until reduced to about 5 tablespoons. Strain and cool.

Sieve the apricot jam into the cooled curry mixture. Whisk in the yogurt. Gradually fold into the chilled mayonnaise. Stir until well blended. Season with a little salt and pepper.

Poach the chickens or turkey in water with the flavouring ingredients. Allow 20 minutes per 500 g/1 lb plus 15 minutes. Test with a skewer. The juices should run clear when cooked. Remove from the liquid and leave to cool. Skin and remove all the flesh. Cut into large strips and place in a bowl with the walnuts. Pour in the mayonnaise and stir until well blended. Cover and refrigerate until required. Not more than 2 to 3 hours.

Arrange the chicken or turkey mayonnaise on a bed of French beans. Garnish with watercress sprigs and orange twists.

HOT CHEESE BREAD

125 g/4 oz Flora margarine
125 g/4 oz low-fat soft cheese
grated rind of 1 lemon
coarsely ground black pepper
1 long crusty loaf
1 long black rye loaf
2 tablespoons grated
Parmesan cheese

Beat together the margarine, soft cheese, lemon rind and pepper.

Thickly slice the two loaves into irregular chunks. Spread the cheese mixture on one side of the bread and sandwich the loaves together again.

Wrap tightly in foil. Bake in a preheated oven (200°C/400°F, Gas Mark 6) for 25 minutes. Serve hot.

An irresistible bread which is very quick to put together and well worth making extra to have on hand in the freezer.

Omit the soft cheese and use grated Edam cheese with 1 tablespoon chopped chives to produce a delicious savoury loaf. Serve hot with main-meal soups for lunch or supper.

Seafood vinaigrette, as economical or as extravagant as you want it to be.

SEAFOOD VINAIGRETTE

250 g/8 oz couscous
750 g/1½ lb monkfish or cod
fillet, skinned
1 bayleaf
250 g/8 oz long-grain
brown rice
500 g/1 lb red peppers, seeded
and roughly chopped
350 g/12 oz spring onions,
finely chopped
350 g/12 oz peeled, cooked
prawns
8 tablespoons chopped fresh
coriander or parsley
a little salt
freshly ground black pepper

VINAIGRETTE
150 ml/¼ pint Flora Oil
50 ml/2 fl oz white wine vinegar
a little salt
freshly ground black pepper
pinch of caster sugar
4 tablespoons chopped
fresh chives

Place the couscous in a large mixing bowl. Cover with enough cold water to come about 5 cm/2 inch above the level of the grains. Leave to soak overnight. Drain well if necessary. The couscous should have absorbed most of the liquid.

Cut the monkfish or cod into bite-size pieces. Place in a saucepan with the bayleaf, cover with cold water and simmer for 12 to 15 minutes, or until just cooked. Drain well and cool.

Cook the rice in plenty of boiling lightly salted water for about 35 minutes until just tender. Drain and stir into the couscous.

Carefully stir the peppers, monkfish, spring onions, prawns and coriander or parsley into the rice and couscous. Season with a little salt and pepper.

To make the vinaigrette, whisk together the ingredients. Stir into the salad mixture. Cover and refrigerate until required. Garnish with coriander sprigs and lemon or lime wedges, before serving.

If couscous is unobtainable make the salad with brown rice, using 500 g/1 lb.

CELEBRATION BUFFET FOR TWELVE	
⊖ medium fibre	1695 calories
⊖ med. saturated fat	P:S ratio 2:1

CHERRY TOMATO SALAD

750 g/1½ lb cherry tomatoes
3 tablespoons Flora Oil
3 tablespoons chopped
fresh basil
3 tablespoons lemon juice
a little salt
freshly ground black pepper
250 g/8 oz pitted black olives

Wash the tomatoes and halve any large ones.

To make the dressing, whisk together the oil, basil, lemon juice and a little salt and pepper. Stir into the tomatoes with the olives. Garnish with fresh basil leaves.

Perfect endings: refreshing Peaches with kiwi fruit and Baked cherry cheesecake.

AVOCADO with GRAPES

2 heads radicchio
3 bunches watercress, trimmed
175 g/6oz bean sprouts
2 firm, ripe avocados
½ cucumber, sliced
175 g/6 oz green grapes, halved
and seeded

DRESSING
150 ml/¼ pint Flora Oil
4 tablespoons white
wine vinegar
1 clove of garlic, crushed
2 tablespoons natural yogurt
a little salt
freshly ground black pepper

Tear the radicchio into bite-size pieces. Wash, drain and pat dry on absorbent kitchen paper. Wash and drain the water-cress and bean sprouts. Mix together and refrigerate in a large polythene bag.

To make the dressing, whisk together the oil, vinegar, garlic and yogurt. Season with a little salt and pepper.

When ready to serve, peel, halve and stone the avocados, and thickly slice into the dressing. Reserve a few slices for garnish. Toss all the remaining ingredients together and serve immediately garnished with the reserved avocado.

PEACHES with KIWI FRUIT

1½ kg/3 lb ripe peaches
6 tablespoons Kirsch
6 tablespoons sparkling
mineral water
1 tablespoon clear honey
3 kiwi fruit
2 passion fruit
toasted flaked almonds, to
decorate (optional)

Halve, stone and thickly slice the peaches. Pour over the Kirsch, water and honey and stir well. Cover and place in the refrigerator to chill for 20 minutes.

Peel and thickly slice the kiwi fruit. Halve the passion fruit and scoop out the pulp. Stir into the peaches. Decorate with toasted flaked almonds if wished.

If peaches are not available use fresh apricots, or mango, or peel and thinly slice 12 small oranges.

For extra special occasions, omit the Kirsch and mineral water and use 200 ml/⅓ pint sparkling white wine or apple juice.

Note: passion fruits are wrinkled, brown mysterious-looking fruits. Once cut open they reveal a bright yellow seed-pulp which has an unusual tart-sweet taste. It is delicious in simple fruit salads such as this.

BAKED CHERRY CHEESECAKE

MAKES 2

125 g/4 oz Flora margarine
125 g/4 oz light brown sugar
500 g/1 lb low-fat soft cheese
2 eggs, separated
50 g/2 oz ground almonds
50 g/2 oz semolina
175 g/6 oz fresh red morello
cherries, stoned and halved or
125 g/4 oz canned pitted
cherries
1 teaspoon icing sugar

Cream together the margarine and sugar until very pale and fluffy. Beat in the cheese and egg yolks until smooth and thoroughly combined. Gradually fold in the ground almonds, semolina, and cherries.

Whisk the egg whites until stiff but not dry and gently fold into the mixture with a metal spoon or spatula.

Lightly oil the base and sides of a deep 20 cm/8 inch round, loose-based flan tin. Spoon in the mixture and bake in a preheated oven (190°/375°F, Gas Mark 5) for about 45 to 50 minutes or until golden brown and just firm to the touch.

Leave to cool in the tin for about 1 hour. (The cheesecake will sink slightly.) Carefully ease out of the tin and slide onto a flat serving plate. Dust with icing sugar and decorate with whole cherries.

SUNDAY LUNCH for SIX

CARROT AND LENTIL SOUP
ROAST BEEF IN RED WINE — YORKSHIRE PUDDING
POTATO AND PARSNIP PURÉE
BRAISED CELERY
PEAR AND GINGER PIE — ORANGE CUSTARD

CARROT and LENTIL SOUP

6 whole green cardamoms
250 g/8 oz carrot, coarsely grated
125 g/4 oz onion, thinly sliced
50 g/2 oz Flora margarine
50 g/2 oz split red lentils
1½ litres/2½ pints chicken stock
1 rasher lean back bacon
a little salt
freshly ground black pepper

Split the cardamoms, remove the seeds and finely crush with a rolling pin. Sauté together the carrot, cardamom and onion in the margarine for 4 to 5 minutes. Stir in the lentils. Cook, stirring, for a further minute.

Add the stock and bacon. Bring to the boil, cover and simmer gently for about 20 minutes or until the lentils are just tender. Remove the bacon and season with a little salt and pepper, if necessary.

Garnish with small shapes of thinly sliced carrots and lime rind or cucumber skin.

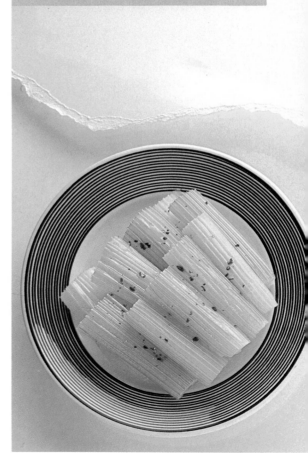

From the left: Braised celery; Potato and parsnip purée; Roast beef in red wine.

YORKSHIRE PUDDING

125 g/4 oz plain or wholemeal flour
a little salt
2 eggs
200 ml/⅓ pint skimmed milk
75 ml/3 fl oz water
3 tablespoons Flora Oil

Place the flour and salt in a bowl. Make a well in the centre and add the eggs and half the liquid. Gradually whisk together to form a smooth batter. Stir in the remaining liquid.

Forty minutes before the meat is cooked, raise the oven temperature to (220°C/425°F, Gas Mark 7). Place the joint lower in the oven. Put the oil in an ovenproof dish, and heat on the top shelf for about 5 to 7 minutes until smoking hot. Quickly pour in the batter. Replace in the oven and cook for about 40 minutes or until risen and crisp.

SUNDAY LUNCH FOR SIX	
◖ medium fibre	1460 calories
◖ med. saturated fat	P:S ratio 3:1

ROAST BEEF in RED WINE

*1½ kg/3 lb piece of rolled
topside
1 clove garlic, halved
1 tablespoon plain flour
1 teaspoon English
mustard powder
200 ml/1⅓ pint red wine*

Wipe the meat. Trim off any excess fat, leaving only a thin covering. Rub the joint with the garlic. Mix together the mustard and flour and rub over the beef. Set the joint on a rack over a roasting tin. Place in a preheated oven (220°C/425°F, Gas Mark 7) for 15 minutes. Lower the heat to (190°C/375°F, Gas Mark 5) and roast for 1 hour for rare, 1¼ hours for well done. Halfway through the cooking time pour all the fat from the pan and pour the wine over the meat. Baste occasionally. At the end of cooking time, strain the pan juices to make the gravy. Garnish the beef with celery leaves.

Wedges of warm Pear and ginger pie
served with Orange custard.

POTATO and PARSNIP PURÉE

1 kg/2 lb parsnips
500 g/1 lb potatoes
a little salt
50 g/2 oz Flora margarine
pinch of ground nutmeg
freshly ground black pepper

Peel the parsnips and potatoes and cut into small chunks. Boil together in lightly salted water until very tender, about 45 minutes. Drain well and mash or sieve.

Return the purée to the saucepan with the margarine, nutmeg and pepper. Cook over a high heat, stirring frequently, until any excess moisture has evaporated. Garnish with chopped parsley and bayleaves.

The purée can also be baked in the oven alongside the Yorkshire Pudding. Fold one egg yolk and two lightly whisked egg whites into the finished purée. Spoon into a lightly greased pie dish. Bake in the preheated oven (220°C/425°F, Gas Mark 7) for 35 to 40 minutes. Cover loosely with foil towards the end of cooking time.

BRAISED CELERY

1¼ kg/2½ lb celery
1 tablespoon Flora Oil
1 bayleaf
300 ml/½ pint chicken stock
a little salt
freshly ground black pepper

Wash the celery then cut into 5 cm/2 inch lengths, reserving any leafy tops for garnish. Heat the oil in a large flameproof casserole. Sauté the celery and bayleaf for 2 minutes. Add the stock and a little salt and pepper. Bring to the boil then cover tightly. Cook in a preheated oven (220°C/425°F, Gas Mark 7) for 20 minutes. (The celery should still retain some bite.) Garnish with coarsely ground black peppercorns.

When fresh herbs are plentiful, add 1 or 2 tablespoons of chopped thyme or sage to the casserole before cooking.

PEAR and GINGER PIE

PASTRY
125 g/4 oz White Flora
250 g/8 oz self-raising flour
1 egg, separated
2 tablespoons water

50 g/2 oz fresh wholemeal breadcrumbs
1 kg/2 lb firm pears
1 tablespoon soft brown sugar
grated rind and juice of 1 orange
½ teaspoon ground ginger

Place the white fat, egg yolk, water and 2 tablespoons of the flour in a bowl and mix together well with a fork. Stir in the remaining flour and mix to a firm dough. Turn out onto a lightly floured surface and knead gently until smooth. Roll out the pastry thinly to a 33 cm/13 inch round. Use to line a 20 cm/8 inch plain flan ring placed on a flat baking sheet. Leave the excess pastry hanging over the edge.

Sprinkle the breadcrumbs onto the pastry base. Peel, core and thickly slice the pears onto the pastry. Add the sugar, orange rind and 2 tablespoons of juice and the ginger. Lift the excess pastry up over the fruit. (It will not completely cover the fruit.) Brush with the lightly beaten egg white. Bake at (190°C/375°F, Gas Mark 5) for 1 hour. Cover lightly with foil if browning too quickly. Slide onto a serving dish and ease off the metal flan ring. Serve warm with Orange Custard.

Note: either wholemeal flour, white flour or a combination of the two can be used to make the pastry.

ORANGE CUSTARD

2 tablespoons cornflour
450 ml/¾ pint pure,
unsweetened orange juice
1 tablespoon soft brown sugar
150 ml/¼ pint natural yogurt

Mix the cornflour to a smooth paste with a little of the orange juice. Bring the remaining juice to the boil. Remove from the heat and whisk in the cornflour mixture and sugar. Return to the boil, stirring all the time until thickened. Remove pan from the heat and whisk the yogurt into the mixture.

Serve warm or chilled.

Any pure, unsweetened fruit juice can be transformed into a light custard in this way. Try adding a pinch of mixed spice and a little honey rather than sugar for a delicious variation.

FORMAL DINNER for SIX

MINTED CARROTS AND COURGETTES
GRATIN OF VEAL
FRENCH BEANS WITH MUSHROOMS
BAKED TOMATOES
RASPBERRY LIQUEUR PUDDING

MINTED CARROTS and COURGETTES

175 g/6 oz carrots
175 g/6 oz courgettes
2 tablespoons chopped
fresh mint
5 tablespoons pure,
unsweetened apple juice
a little salt
freshly ground black pepper

Pare and discard the outer skin of the carrots. Continue paring the carrots into wafer-thin strips until as much as possible of each carrot has been used.

Trim the courgettes. Pare into wafer-thin strips as for the carrots. Mix the vegetables together and cover with cold water. Chill for 30 minutes.

Whisk together the mint, apple juice and a little salt and pepper. Drain the vegetables. Toss in the dressing and serve immediately, garnished with fresh mint sprigs.

This is a stunningly simple and impressive starter. The wafer thin strips of vegetables look particularly attractive when served on flat white plates.

GRATIN of VEAL

2 tablespoons Flora Oil
50 g/2 oz onion, chopped
6 black olives, pitted
and chopped
198 g/7 oz can tuna fish, in
brine, drained
50 g/2 oz fresh wholemeal
breadcrumbs
2 tablespoons wine vinegar
6 veal escalopes
50 g/2 oz Flora margarine
4 tablespoons plain flour
600 ml/1 pint skimmed milk
175 g/6 oz low-fat soft cheese
1 tablespoon grated
Parmesan cheese

Heat 1 tablespoon of the oil in a sauté pan. Sauté the onion and olives for 1 to 2 minutes. Stir in the tuna fish and breadcrumbs. Remove pan from the heat and add the vinegar and a little salt and pepper. Cool.

Place the veal escalopes between two layers of cling film and beat out very thinly (or get the butcher to do it for you). Divide the fish mixture between the escalopes and fold and roll to form neat parcels. Tie securely with fine string.

Brown the veal parcels well in the remaining oil. Remove the string and place the parcels, seam side down, in a shallow casserole.

Melt the margarine in a saucepan. Stir in the flour and cook for 1 minute. Stir in the milk. Bring to the boil. Simmer for 1 minute. Remove pan from the heat, beat in the soft cheese and Parmesan and season with a little salt and pepper.

Pour the sauce over the veal. Cover and cook in a preheated oven (180°C/350°F, Gas Mark 4) for 45 minutes. Garnish with black olives and watercress. Serve on a bed of cooked tagliatelle.

Allow about 700 g/1½ lb of fresh tagliatelle per person or 350 g/12 oz dried.

FORMAL DINNER FOR SIX
◖ medium fibre   660 calories
● low saturated fat   P:S ratio 0.5:1

BAKED TOMATOES

12 small, firm tomatoes, about
1 kg/2 lb in total weight
2 tablespoons white
wine vinegar
a little salt
1 teaspoon coarsely ground
black pepper

Make a small cross in the bottom of each tomato. Place stalk end down in a shallow ovenproof dish. Pour over the vinegar and enough water to come 5 mm/¼ inch up the sides of the dish. Season with a little salt and sprinkle over the black pepper.

Bake in a preheated oven (180°C/350°F, Gas Mark 4) for 15 to 20 minutes. Garnish with fresh marjoram or mint sprigs.

Baked tomatoes make a quick, colourful addition to any meal. Choose even-sized, firm tomatoes for best results. Test with a skewer after 15 minutes. They should be just cooked but not too soft.

Baked tomatoes; Gratin of veal; French beans; Minted carrots & courgettes.

FRENCH BEANS with MUSHROOMS

250 g/8 oz French beans,
topped and tailed
250 g/8 oz button mushrooms
grated rind and juice of 1 lemon
1 tablespoon pine nuts
a little salt
freshly ground black pepper

Cook the beans in boiling, salted water for 5 minutes. Drain and rinse under cold water. Place the beans and mushrooms in a lightly greased ovenproof dish. Stir in the lemon rind and juice, pine nuts and a little salt and pepper.

Cover tightly with foil. Bake in a preheated oven (180°C/350°F, Gas Mark 4) for about 35 to 45 minutes. The beans should still retain some bite.

If pine nuts are unobtainable use 1 tablespoon toasted, flaked almonds.

RASPBERRY LIQUEUR PUDDING

500 g/1 lb blackcurrants,
fresh or frozen
500 g/1 lb raspberries,
fresh or frozen
150 ml/¼ pint medium
white wine
50 ml/2 fl oz Crème de Cassis
3 tablespoons soft brown sugar
250 g/8 oz sliced white or
wholemeal bread
1 egg white
pinch ground cinnamon
150 ml/¼ pint natural yogurt

Thaw the fruit if necessary. Place in a saucepan with the wine and Crème de Cassis. Bring slowly to the boil, stir in 2 tablespoons of the sugar and remove from heat. Cool.

Remove the crusts from the bread. Use one slice to cover the base of a 1½ litre/2½ pint pudding basin. Spoon over a little of the fruit mixture. Continue layering the fruit and bread with all but 2 tablespoons of the fruit mixture, ending with a slice of bread.

Place a small plate on top of the mixture. Weight down and refrigerate overnight.

To serve, loosen the sides of the pudding with a palette knife. Invert onto a serving plate. Brush over reserved juices to completely stain the bread. Decorate with whole fruit and mint sprigs or raspberry leaves.

Stiffly whisk the egg white. Whisk in the remaining sugar and cinnamon. Fold into the yogurt and serve with the pudding.

Alternatively cut the pudding into wedges and serve on a bed of raspberry leaves. Decorate with whole fruit and serve with the cinnamon yogurt.

Making the most of soft, summer fruits:
Raspberry liqueur pudding.

SUPPER PARTY for SIX

WALNUT YOGURT DIP
AVOCADO CHEESE – CRUDITÉS
DRUNKEN PHEASANT
VEGETABLE PLATTER – BRAISED PUMPKIN
PASSION FRUIT PAVLOVA

WALNUT YOGURT DIP

50 g/2 oz ground walnuts
1 clove garlic, crushed
1 teaspoon Flora Oil
1 teaspoon lemon juice
150 ml/¼ pint natural yogurt
a little salt
50 g/2 oz cucumber, peeled and finely chopped

Beat together the walnuts, garlic, oil and lemon juice. Gradually stir in the yogurt. Season with a little salt. Cover and refrigerate until required. Just before serving stir the cucumber into the yogurt mixture.

Serve chilled with a selection of crisp fresh vegetables such as:

matchstick lengths of carrot, courgette and celery

strips of yellow and green pepper

small button mushrooms

small cauliflower florets

For a stiffer mixture, omit the natural yogurt and use 125 g/4 oz low-fat soft cheese or natural quark.

AVOCADO CHEESE

1 very ripe avocado pear
1 tablespoon lemon juice
1 clove garlic, crushed
¼ onion, grated
50 g/2 oz low-fat soft cheese, or natural quark
a little salt
freshly ground black pepper
1 tomato, skinned, seeded and finely chopped

Peel the avocado, halve and remove the stone. Mash with the lemon juice until smooth. Beat in the garlic, onion, cheese and a little salt and pepper. Serve chilled, sprinkled with the chopped tomato, and accompanied by Melba toast.

To make Melba toast: lightly toast 3 slices of wholemeal bread under the grill. While still warm, remove the crusts and split the bread in half horizontally. Cut each half into four triangles. Lightly toast the uncooked side of the bread until golden and beginning to curl. Cool and store in an airtight container until required.

Alternatively, serve finger lengths of warm pitta bread.

SUPPER PARTY FOR SIX	
◖ medium fibre	1105 calories
● low saturated fat	P:S ratio 2:1

VEGETABLE PLATTER

750 g/1½ lb small new potatoes
250 g/8 oz mangetout
topped and tailed
a little salt
freshly ground black pepper
25 g/1 oz Flora margarine

Wash the potatoes well (peel if necessary). Halve any large ones. Place in a large metal colander or steamer set over a pan of boiling water. Cover tightly with foil and steam for 12 minutes.

Uncover, add the mangetout. Cover and steam for a further 4 to 5 minutes or until both vegetables are just cooked. Season with a little salt and pepper and toss in the margarine before serving on a heated platter or arranged around the pheasants.

BRAISED PUMPKIN

1 kg/2 lb pumpkin, peeled and
seeds removed
juice of 1 lemon
2 tablespoons Flora Oil
pinch of dried oregano
150 ml/¼ pint chicken stock
a little salt
freshly ground black pepper

Cut the pumpkin into finger-size pieces. Sprinkle with the lemon juice and leave to stand for 5 minutes.

Heat the oil in a large sauté pan and sauté the pumpkin for 3 to 4 minutes, or until beginning to brown. Add the oregano, stock and a little salt and pepper.

Cover and simmer over a low heat for 10 to 15 minutes or until the pumpkin is just tender.

If pumpkin is unobtainable, substitute celeriac, turnip or Jerusalem artichokes.

DRUNKEN PHEASANT

50 g/2 oz Flora margarine
3 small pheasants
a little salt
freshly ground black pepper
8 juniper berries, crushed
3 rashers lean back
bacon, rinded
600 ml/1 pint dry cider
300 ml/½ pint chicken stock
2 tablespoons plain white flour
3 tablespoons gin
grated rind and juice of 1 orange
1 tablespoon redcurrant or
cranberry jelly

Spread the margarine over the pheasants. Place in a large casserole and season with a little salt and pepper. Sprinkle with the juniper berries. Stretch the bacon with the back of a knife and place one rasher over each bird.

Pour over the cider. Cover and cook in a preheated oven (200°C/400°F, Gas Mark 6) for 50 to 60 minutes, or until the pheasants are tender and cooked through.

Remove the birds to a warmed serving dish and keep warm. Skim off any fat from the casserole liquid then whisk in the flour. Continue whisking and add the stock, gin, orange rind, 3 tablespoons orange juice and the redcurrant or cranberry jelly. Bring to the boil and simmer for 2 to 3 minutes.

Carve or simply halve the pheasants. Garnish with watercress sprigs, twists of orange and orange needleshreds. Strain the gravy into a warmed sauce boat and serve.

Drunken pheasant; Braised pumpkin;
Walnut yogurt dip; Avocado cheese.

PASSION FRUIT PAVLOVA

3 egg whites
175 g/6 oz soft brown sugar
2 teaspoons cornflour
2 teaspoons white wine vinegar
¼ teaspoon vanilla essence

TOPPING
250 g/8 oz low-fat soft cheese
150 ml/¼ pint natural yogurt
2 tablespoons clear honey
1 banana, sliced thinly
2 nectarines, sliced
*2 ripe mangoes, peeled
and sliced*
2 passion fruit

Whisk the egg whites until stiff then gradually whisk in the sugar until the meringue is very stiff. Whisk in the cornflour, vinegar and vanilla essence.

Pile the meringue onto a baking sheet lined with non-stick baking parchment and spread into a 20 cm/8 inch round. Hollow out the centre slightly and bake in a preheated oven (150°C/300°F, Gas Mark 2) for 1½ hours.

Cool, then remove the paper and place the Pavlova on a serving dish (it will crack slightly but this is characteristic of a Pavlova).

Mix the cheese with the yogurt and honey then fold in the banana. Pile onto the meringue and decorate with the nectarines and mango. Halve the passion fruit and scoop out the pulp. Scatter over the top.

Pavlova is also delicious if filled with peeled and chopped pineapple and scoops of Brown Bread Ice Cream (see page 40).

A Glossary of Flour

Our most common flour is made from the wheat grain. This consists of an outer covering of 'bran' with an inner 'endosperm' and 'wheatgerm'. These are all separated during milling and for white flour only the endosperm is used. The term *extraction* found on labels indicates the proportion of the grain which ends up in the flour.

White flours usually contain 72-74 per cent of the wheat grain. They are creamy coloured when freshly milled but many are chemically bleached. Those which are not, are marked 'unbleached' on the pack.

Brown or wheatmeal flours usually contain 85-90 per cent of the wheat grain. The darkness of the flour depends on the amount of bran and wheatgerm present. The more bran, the darker the flour.

Wholemeal Flour is 100 per cent extraction as all the grain is used. Although many people confuse the term 'wheatmeal' with 'wholemeal' they are not the same.

Stoneground flours are milled in the traditional way by grinding the cleaned grain between two grooved stones. All of the constituents of the grain are present and it is therefore 100 per cent extraction.

The principal nutritional difference between flours of various extraction rates is their dietary fibre content. Fibre in the form of bran is removed from white flour. Choosing brown, wheatmeal or wholemeal flour is one simple way of incorporating more fibre and greater variety of colour, flavour and texture into your cooking.

Brown, wheatmeal and wholemeal flours can be bought coarse, medium or fine-milled. The fine-milled varieties are especially good to use in sauces, cakes and pastries as they give more fibre and flavour than white flour.

Flours are also categorized into 'strong' and 'soft', and the degree of strength will depend on the wheat from which they are made.

Strong flours have a high protein and low starch content and should be chosen for recipes requiring a large volume and a strong open texture, e.g. bread and other yeasted doughs, choux, puff and flaky pastries.

Soft flours have a low protein and high starch content and are milled from a very soft wheat, ideal for use in cakes, biscuits and shortcrust pastries where less volume and a softer less open texture is required.

In addition to those mentioned several other flours and meals are available, e.g.:

Buckwheat flour – a coarse, speckled flour which adds a wonderful, nutty flavour to breads and batters (see Breakfast Pancakes page 18).

Rye flour – a flour which ranges in colour from dark to light brown. Used alone it produces a rather, close-textured bread but mixed with a proportion of wholemeal flour it gives a rich, moist result (see Rye and Onion Bread page 46).

Oatmeal – this is a fine creamy-coloured meal which can be bought fine, medium or coarse-milled and used in breads, cakes, biscuits and of course porridge (see page 17).

Which yeast?

Compressed (or fresh) yeast is usually the easiest for the beginner to work with. It is creamy-beige in colour with a firm crumbly texture and looks rather like putty. It is best when really fresh, so buy in small quantities and use as soon as possible. Healthfood shops and bakers who bake on the premises are the most likely stockists. Store in the refrigerator in a polythene bag. Alternatively it

Top to bottom: Buckwheat flour, Wholemeal flour, Wheat bran, Oatmeal.

BACK to BASICS

freezes well but allow to thaw for 30 minutes before using.

Fresh yeast is sometimes rubbed directly into the flour but it is more often blended with liquid before being added. Don't cream fresh yeast with sugar as this inhibits its action.

Dried Yeast is available in two types: **Traditional** (or active dried yeast) comes as small beige granules. It's usually sprinkled into warm water containing a little sugar and left for 15 minutes until frothy. Generally speaking, one tablespoon of dried yeast has the same effect as 25g/1oz of fresh yeast.

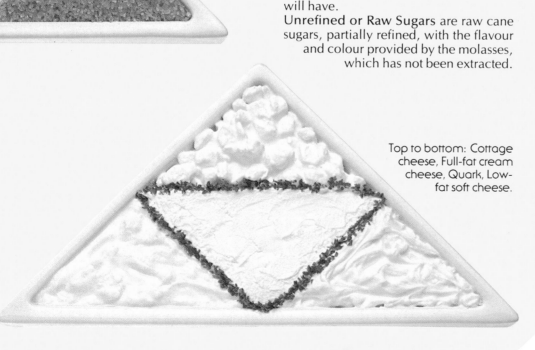

Top to bottom: Muscovado sugar, Demerara sugar, Granulated sugar, Soft brown sugar.

Dried yeast keeps for six months in a cool, dry place. If stale, yeast will have lost it's potency. If it fails to froth while being reconstituted, don't use it.

Easy-mix dried yeast is a fine powder that can be mixed with the flour before liquid is added. It comes in vacuum-sealed sachets, and if only part of it is needed, the rest should be used up within a day or two. One sachet of dried yeast is equivalent to 25g/1oz of fresh.

Sweetenings

Sugar is a food occurring in plants. It is extracted from both sugar cane and sugar beet and there is no significant difference between the white sugar extracted from either of them. There are three main categories of sugar.

White Sugar is one of the purest foods known to man, being 99% pure. It is cleaned to remove all impurities and contains no other nutrients or additives.

Brown Sugar is normally made by adding cane molasses to white sugar, giving it its colour and flavour. Generally the darker the colour the more flavour it will have.

Unrefined or Raw Sugars are raw cane sugars, partially refined, with the flavour and colour provided by the molasses, which has not been extracted.

Top to bottom: Cottage cheese, Full-fat cream cheese, Quark, Low-fat soft cheese.

Honey is a popular and pleasant food, consisting normally of about 75% sugar and most of the remainder is water.

Soft Cheese Summary

Lower-fat soft cheeses with their varying range of tastes and textures are fast becoming some of the most versatile kitchen ingredients in the move towards a lighter style of cooking. These cheeses are the stapel ingredients in many recipes throughout this book. They contribute a light, creamy texture and dairy flavour with only a fraction of the fat of medium and full-fat cheeses and cream.

Soft Cheeses are defined and labelled according to the amount of milk fat and water they contain.

Skimmed Milk Soft Cheese is a soft cheese with less than 2% milk fat and not more than 80% water. It is the lowest in calories, soft, smooth and very light in colour. Examples are skimmed milk, Quark and a range of supermarket own brands. This is very popular in Germany, accounting for about half the total cheese consumption.

Low Fat Soft Cheese is a soft cheese with 2-10% milk fat and up to 80% water.

There are many varieties including Cottage cheese and Crowdie (the Scottish version with a fine texture) and Quark, similar to Cottage cheese but with a smoother texture.

Full Fat Cream Cheese is a soft cheese containing at least 20% milk fat and not more than 60% water. It is usually labelled full fat.

Lower-Fat Hard Cheeses

Lower-fat versions of hard cheeses are now being produced, made with semi-skimmed milk instead of full-fat milk.

Although the amount of fat has been trimmed down, lower-fat hard cheeses still contain more fat than cottage cheese, Quark and skimmed milk, soft cheese; they have a little less fat than Edam, Feta, Ricotta and medium-fat soft cheeses such as Brie, Camembert, Mozzarella and curd cheese.

White Sauce (coating)

White or wholemeal flour may be used. Wholemeal flour gives a very creamy and slightly speckled sauce. For best results use a fine-milled wholemeal flour.

25 g/1 oz Flora margarine
25 g/1 oz plain flour
300 ml/½ pint skimmed milk
a little salt
freshly ground black pepper

Melt the margarine in a small saucepan. Stir in the flour. Cook, stirring for 1 to 2 minutes before adding the milk. Bring to the boil and simmer for 2 to 3 minutes until thickened and smooth.

All-in-One Method

Place all ingredients in a saucepan. Whisking continuously over a moderate heat, bring to the boil and cook for 2 to 3 minutes until thickened and smooth.

Variations (for sweet sauces omit salt and pepper):

Cheese Sauce

50 g/2 oz Edam cheese, grated
½ teaspoon made English mustard

Beat the cheese and mustard into the white sauce, off the heat.

Mushroom Sauce

50 g/2 oz button mushrooms, sliced

Sauté the mushrooms in the margarine before adding the remaining ingredients.

Orange Sauce

Rind and juice of 1 orange
1 tablespoon caster sugar

Beat the rind and juice of orange and the sugar into the white sauce. Serve hot.

Vanilla Sauce

Few drops of vanilla essence
Grated rind of 1 small lemon

Beat the vanilla essence, lemon rind and sugar into the white sauce. Serve hot or cold.

Basic Shortcrust Pastry

125 g/4 oz White Flora
3 tablespoons water
250 g/8 oz plain white flour
a little salt

Place the White Flora in a bowl with the water and 2 tablespoons of the flour. Cream together with a fork until well mixed. Add the remaining flour and continue mixing with a fork to form a firm dough.

Knead thoroughly on a lightly floured surface until firm and smooth.

(For slightly richer pastry use half White Flora and half Flora margarine.)

Wholemeal Shortcrust Pastry

Follow the recipe for Basic Shortcrust Pastry using all plain wholemeal flour, or half plain wholemeal and half plain white, with 4 tablespoons of water.

Choux Pastry

50 g/2 oz Flora margarine
150 ml/¼ pint water
8 tablespoons plain flour
2 eggs, lightly beaten

Melt the margarine in the water and bring to the boil; remove from the heat and quickly tip in the flour all at once. Beat with a wooden spoon until the paste is smooth and forms a ball in the centre of the pan. (Take care not to over-beat.)

Cool slightly before beating in the eggs a little at a time. Beat until smooth. The usual oven setting is (220°C/425°F, Gas Mark 7).

Wholemeal Choux Pastry

Use half plain white and half wholemeal flour.

Right, left to right: Cheese sauce, Mushroom sauce, Orange sauce.

French Dressing

150 ml/¼ pint Flora Oil
5 tablespoons white wine vinegar
a little salt
freshly ground black pepper
½ teaspoon made mustard

Place all the ingredients in a screw-topped jar and shake well. Store in the refrigerator and use as required.

Variations: Use red wine vinegar in place of white wine vinegar.

Add 1 clove garlic, peeled and crushed, and 1 tablespoon ground turmeric.

Add 1 tablespoon chopped fresh herbs.

Add 1 tablespoon toasted sesame seeds.

Left, left to right: Home-made soft cheese, Smetana, Herb cheese.

Mayonnaise

1 egg yolk
½ teaspoon English mustard powder
½ teaspoon caster sugar
1 tablespoon white wine vinegar
200 ml/⅓ pint Flora Oil
4 tablespoons natural yogurt
a little salt
freshly ground black pepper

Place the egg yolk in a medium bowl. Whisk in the mustard, sugar and vinegar. Add the oil, in a thin stream, beating all the time until very thick and smooth. Fold in the yogurt and season lightly. Cover with damp greaseproof paper or cling-film and refrigerate. Mayonnaise will keep for at least two weeks in the refrigerator.

Variations: Use 1 tablespoon wholegrain mustard in place of English mustard powder.

Add 1 to 2 tablespoons chopped fresh herbs e.g. parsley, chives, dill.

Add the grated rind and juice of 1 small lemon.

Home-made Soft Cheese

600 ml/1 pint pasteurized skimmed milk
1 tablespoon skimmed milk powder
25 g/1 oz medium-fat curd cheese
6 drops of rennet

Bring the milk to the boil. Remove from the heat and leave to cool slightly until just warm.

Stir in the skimmed milk powder, curd cheese and rennet. Pour the mixture into a warmed vacuum flask, seal and leave in a warm place for about 8 hours until thickened.

Tip the mixture into a sieve lined with muslin. Leave to drain for 3 to 4 hours or until firm. Store in the refrigerator until ready to use.

Variation: Stir in 2 tablespoons chopped mixed herbs, and 1 clove garlic, crushed.

Home-made Smetana

Smetana is similar in texture and flavour to soured cream but is cultured on low-fat dairy produce.

300 ml/½ pint single cream
300 ml/½ pint skimmed milk
2 tablespoons smetana or soured cream

Mix together the cream and milk and heat gently until just warm. Whisk in the smetana or soured cream. Pour the mixture into a wide-mouthed vacuum flask or yogurt maker. Leave in a warm place for 4 to 5 hours until set. Place in the refrigerator where it will thicken further as it chills.

Left, left to right: Herb dressing, Garlic and turmeric dressing, Mayonnaise.

INDEX

EATING and HEALTH

Answers to the quiz on page 9.

1 b) Both a) and c) should be increased.

2 a) and c) are high in saturated fat. b) and d) are low in saturated fat.

3 c) and d).

4 All three factors and diet increase the risk of heart disease and other related disorders.

5 a) Carrots contain vitamin A which helps our eyes to see in dim light. There is no conclusive evidence that large doses of vitamin C will prevent, or cure, the common cold.

6 b) dried beans.

7 False. Energy is provided from all the food we eat, not just sugar. A sandwich for example will re-fuel the body mid-morning just as efficiently as a Danish pastry or a bar of chocolate.

8 b) and c). Remember that only plant foods have dietary fibre. Ensuring an adequate supply of dietary fibre doesn't mean 'bran with everything'. Adding bran to food (breakfast cereals, cakes, bread, etc.) is fine if you enjoy it but it only provides one form of fibre. There are many tasty ways of ensuring an adequate intake of fibre in all its forms. We should include plenty of fresh fruit and vegetables and more cereals, peas, beans and lentils in our diet.

9 No. No foods help the body to use up fat more quickly.

10 False. Bread, potatoes and pasta are not very high in calories. It's often the extra hard margarine, butter, cream and rich, cheese sauces which pile on the extra calories, and the pounds. Switch to low-fat cheese, yogurt, or vegetable-based sauces.

NOTES

WEIGHTS and MEASURES

Recipes give Metric and Imperial measures. In order to achieve complete success it is important to follow one set of measures only.

All spoons are level measurement. Standard spoon measures are used in all recipes; 1 tablespoon equals 15ml spoon, 1 teaspoon equals 5ml spoon.

INGREDIENTS

All yogurt used is the low-fat variety

All white flour should be sieved

Where simply 'plain' or 'self-raising' flour is stated, either white or wholemeal flour may be used

All canned foods are drained unless otherwise stated

All eggs are size 3 or 4 (standard)

If fresh herbs are unobtainable, substitute dried herbs but halve the quantities stated.

NUTRITION INFORMATION

Fibre and fat content, calories and P:S Ratio are given per single serving of recipe or menu.

Fibre:
- ● more than 4g
- ◒ less than 4g but more than 1g
- ○ less than 1g

Fat:
- ● less than 10% of calories provided by saturated fat
- ◒ more than 10% but less than 25% of calories provided by saturated fat
- ○ more than 25% of calories provided by saturated fat

P:S Ratio:
Besides recommending a reduction in the amount of saturated fat in the diet, many international medical committees which have made dietary recommendations for the prevention of coronary heart disease have advocated a Polyunsaturated/Saturated Fats ratio of towards 1. The idea is to substitute polyunsaturated fats to balance the amount of saturated fats in the diet.

As a guide to using this book, therefore, choose freely from dishes with a P:S ratio of 1 or more. If a dish has a P:S ratio of less than one, combine it with another with a P:S ratio of more than one to achieve a balance between the two types of fat.